LOST
BUT
NEVER ALONE

MaryAnn Westgard

 FriesenPress

Suite 300 - 990 Fort St
Victoria, BC, V8V 3K2
Canada

www.friesenpress.com

Copyright © 2021 by MaryAnn Westgard
First Edition — 2021

ISBN
978-1-03-910568-3 (Hardcover)
978-1-03-910567-6 (Paperback)
978-1-03-910569-0 (eBook)

1. Biography & Autobiography, Women

Distributed to the trade by The Ingram Book Company

TABLE OF CONTENTS

CHAPTER 1

In the beginning

I was born 'MaryAnn Elizabeth McLean', third child of William McLean and Ilyne Maybelle, nee Larson, on February 18,1944. I am told that my Dad was away at a curling bonspiel when my mother went into labour. She called a cab to take her to Saskatoon City Hospital and I was almost born in the taxi. This is not surprising since patience is not one of my better virtues. I was, however, born minutes or seconds later in the hospital.

I started out my life as a very precious part of the family, since I was the first girl after two boys (Robert Stuart and Donald Lionel). My first memories are of being very loved and wanted. My Father was in road construction which took him away from home for long periods of time. My Mother however was a stay-at home Mom. For this reason, I naturally gravitated to my Mother who was always there for me and made me feel loved and cherished.

In 1951 my sister Sylvia Ilyne was born completing our family of two boys and then two girls. I was so happy to have a sister and I loved her dearly even though she was many years my junior.

I was a very shy girl always wanting to please everyone. I think that was because my Dad was an alcoholic and the repercussions were that the whole family suffered as a result. I don't ever remember doing anything as a family, we were different. Compared to other families we were very poor because Dad usually spent most of his pay cheque on treating his cronies in the bar after work. Mom never got to see much of his pay cheque and she was always struggling to put food on the table and pay the rent. Because of his job in road construction, he was away a lot and I must say that I liked those times best because when he was home there seemed to be a lot of tension. When he drank which was most of the time, he got irritable and sometimes violent. His temper could flare at the drop of a hat, putting everyone on edge. When he was home, I tried to stay out of his way as much as possible.

My Mother always took the brunt of his wrath because she was always asking for more money for food and bills. She couldn't make do with what he was giving her. When he was home, he would go to the bar and when it closed, he would bring one or two guys home with him, and get Mom out of bed to cook a meal for them. Of course, this was playing the big shot with his friends. When Dad was home, he expected steak, real butter, maraschino cherry chocolates and ice cream. If Mom didn't have it, she was in real trouble. When Dad left our only meat was a few wieners and white margarine that we had to colour ourselves. Sometimes Mom would make poor-man's porridge that was basically flour, water and a little sugar. Things were really tough for us but Mom being the good cook that she was always seemed to pull something together. Sometimes neighbours would give Mom vegetables from their garden and we would get hand-me-down clothes from people. Through all of this, Mom would put on a happy face, take us to church and Sunday school, she even played piano for the services. We never let on to anyone about what was going on at home. It was natural to hide things and pretend that all was normal when in fact we knew that things were very far from normal. Our family was different, very different.

CHAPTER 2

The early years

I grew up with no grandmothers or grandfathers to influence my life. My grandfather on my mom's side (Gus Larson) farmed just outside of Outlook, Saskatchewan in the summer time and then spent his winters in Vancouver for the milder climate. My grandfather on my dad's side (Robert McLean) had died 9 years before I was born. My grandmother on my mom's side (Indiana Constance (Dahl) Larson had died when my mother was only six years old. She died in the 1918 pandemic that swept across the world killing fifty million people worldwide. She was twenty-eight years old at the time and had just given birth to her sixth child when she died. My grandmother (Mary (Harrow) McLean) on my dad's side died when I was three years old. She had been riding with my Dad in his truck and at that time there was no such thing as seatbelts. He turned a corner and her door flew open and she fell out, landing on the curb and breaking her back. From then on, she was bed ridden and my Mom looked after her. Being that I was only three years old, I have very little recollection of her. I have been told, however, about a story that happened shortly before her death.

I guess my brother Don would have been about six years old at the time. He had taken some of his older brother's comic books that he wasn't supposed to have. So that he wouldn't be seen, he took the comic books and some matches which Dad had left by his cigarettes, and went under his bed to read the comic books. Upon lighting a match to see the comic, it quickly burned down to his fingers and he dropped the match which immediately started to burn the comic. He got scared and didn't know what to do so he got out from under the bed, shut the door to the bedroom and then went out to the living room and sat down as if nothing had happened. His face as white as a ghost for fear of the consequences. A short time later Mom and Dad smelled smoke and went to see where it was coming from. Grandma shouted from her bedroom that she had smelled smoke. One of her biggest fears was fire because she was bed ridden and couldn't walk. Mom went to assure Grandma that the smoke was from something she burned on the stove and nothing to worry about. Then Mom and Dad went into high gear. By now the curtains were on fire as well as the bed. Dad broke the window and ripped down the burning curtains and then threw them out the broken window. Next, they shoved the burning mattress out the window. Outside they watered everything down with a hose and were able to stop what might have been an extreme tragedy.

Another story that I remember happened when I was about five years old. I know that I wasn't in school yet. It was summer time and because my brothers had no school, we spent the summer with Dad in his camp. You see, he was in road construction and that was the only time that we could go with him. We lived in a trailer or as they called it, a caboose. Mom would cook for the crew while we were there. One day Mom had me sitting up on the table and she was putting curlers in my hair. Suddenly there was a crash and she and I both went sailing across the room. I remember it like it was yesterday. There was so much commotion as everyone came running to see if we were okay. Apparently, a large earth mover, with tires taller than a man, had been left idling on the top of a hill, it slipped into gear and came tearing down the hill shearing off the whole front end of our caboose. That was really a close call but I will have many more before this life is done.

When I started school in grade one, I was subject to many other kids and the regular childhood diseases that go along with that. I especially remember getting the measles and I was extremely sick with a very high fever. Going to the hospital was not an option for us because we were very poor and there was no free health care then. I remember Mom mopping my forehead with cold cloths to try and bring down the fever. What I remember most is what came next, for my next recollection was of me floating in the air with my back against the ceiling looking down on myself laying on the sofa with Mom earnestly praying for my welfare. I don't know how long this actually was but at some point, I found myself back in my body and I felt a whole lot better. I heard Mom say that my fever was breaking. Mom said that God answered her prayers that day. Later as an adult I found out that I had had an out of body experience. You see, my mother was a very Godly woman and I remember that at an early age I loved the Lord too. Mom played piano at the church services and I, along with my brothers, went to Sunday School. Mom did her best to raise us right.

I remember one time, I think that I was in grade one at the time, I had come in from playing outside and Mom was sitting at the table crying. I had never seen my mother cry before so I was very concerned and asked what was wrong.

She said she had no food for supper and didn't know what to do. I figured that I had to do something because my mom was hurting bad, so I took a shopping bag, the old kind made of heavy paper with handles on the top. I figured that I would have to weigh it down with something or the store clerks would think it funny if I came into the store with an empty bag, went out with a full one, and never went through the check out. An old rag tag doll is what I used. I knew it was wrong but I thought God would approve since it was an emergency.

So off I went to get Mom some groceries for supper. The store was only a block away. Looking back on this event I don't know how I got away with it. It was like I was invisible or something. I walked into the store and proceeded filling up my bag till I could hardly carry it, with things that caught my eye, probably not the things Mom would have picked. I remember getting bananas, cheese, a coconut in the shell (because I had seen some other kids eating that and I wondered what it was like), and wieners but I don't remember what else I got that day. I walked out of that store with my bag full of groceries and no one stopped me. I only know that I could hardly carry that bag and sometimes I dragged it a bit but I finally got it home. Mom, of course, asked where I had gotten it from and I didn't think God would mind me telling a fib this one time, so I said a woman on the next block had asked if we needed some extra food because she had too much, and I said sure. Being that Mom was so desperate, she didn't ask any more questions and we had a really different kind of exotic meal that night. At least it put a smile on Mom's face again.

As I was growing up, I absolutely adored my two older brothers. They were my heroes and I knew that if anyone tried to bully me, they would be right there to protect me.

As a result of my fondness for them and the fact that they always seemed to be having so much fun, I wanted to go everywhere they went and do what they did. This resulted in me becoming quite the tomboy as I tagged along.

One such experience almost resulted in tragedy. My brothers and two other friends decided to cross the old train trestle bridge from the underside. They dared each other to cross over to the other side and then come back from the underside. Of course, no one wanted to be a chicken and not go. I was told to wait on the riverbank and that they wouldn't be long. I was six or seven years old at the time. My brothers would have been about nine and twelve. None of us should have been hanging out at the river, but here we were and I was not to be outdone by my brothers. I waited a bit but then decided I would go too. The boys never noticed me because they were concentrating heavily on what they were doing. One slip and they would fall to the raging river below.

The boys were a lot faster than I was with my shorter legs and arms. It was very scary because it was a very long way down to the water and I knew that if I fell that would be the end of me since I could only dog paddle a bit but certainly not enough to get me out of that swift current and to safety. I was about halfway across and the boys were nearly at the other shore when we heard the train. The boys rushed to the other side and got off the bridge. That's when they noticed me and started yelling to me to hang on and to dare not let go.

They were helplessly looking on from a distance. As soon as the train started on to the bridge, the bridge shook terribly but when the train was over top of me on the bridge it was dripping something—not sure if it was oil or water since it was an old steam engine not like the trains today. I had all I could do to hang on with the shaking and the burning from the hot liquid drops on my skin, but letting go was not an option. Finally, when I thought that I couldn't take it any more, the train was finally gone and the bridge stopped shaking. My arms were covered with blisters from the hot liquid and by now I was shaking, I think from shock. That's when the boys reached me and helped me back to shore. I was given quite the lecture about not telling Mom what really happened but rather that I had had a brush with poison ivy or something which caused the blisters on my skin. I don't think Mom ever knew the real truth about what happened that day.

Summers were my best time of year because if I was lucky, I would have a chance to get out of the city for a while. My cousin Carmen, at that time, lived on a farm just north of Broderick. While she pined about coming to the city, I pined for the farm life. I could never understand what good she saw about city life and she never understood why I would want to come to the farm. It was on one such trip to the farm that the next story begins.

It was a beautiful summer's day and I was at my favourite place, visiting my cousins at their farm. I loved the sights and sounds of nature, the freedom from the city and the wide-open spaces. It got to be pretty hot that day so my cousins were begging their dad, my uncle Ernie, to take us down to the river so we could swim. He obliged and put cousin Dorelle in charge because she was the oldest. Dorelle was twelve or thirteen, Carmen six, and I was about eight. There was a nice sandy beach and the water was fairly shallow making things look pretty safe. However, Uncle Ernie gave us strict orders not to go past a certain point in the shoreline because there was an intake pipe that pumped water out of the river to who knows where.

Anyway, kids being kids, and me the better swimmer of the three, I ended up too far downstream and before I knew what had happened, I was sucked underwater and was caught on something. I was thrashing around and as my arms were going up, I felt the top of what I believed to be cribbing, like the inside of a well. I grabbed a hold and pulled myself up so my head was out of the water and I was crouched on top of the cribbing, crying, shaking and scared stiff. Dorelle was hollering from the shore, she said, "jump as far as you can and swim as hard as you can, it's your only chance to get away from the water pulling you back in."

I did what she said and made it to shore. Luckily, I was a pretty good swimmer by this time. When I got out of the water, we realized that my bathing suit was torn right down to the elastic around my leg and that is what had saved me. When I was thrashing around under the water, I had felt a large spike (nail) on the inside of the cribbing. My suit had caught on that spike, tore down to the elastic around my leg and held me till I felt the top of the cribbing and pulled myself up. There was such a force sucking me down and I would have surely died, but someone (God) was certainly looking out for me that day.

I remember being so envious of other kids at school especially in the fall when they came back from their holidays. Many had gone to camp and they were giving a play by play of all the things they did. It sounded like so much fun as they would be reliving times at the lake, boating, water skiing, etc., with family and friends. I wanted so badly to do the things the other kids got to do but we were not a family that did things together and besides we could never afford to do those things anyway.

As Dad's drinking progressed other problems arose. We were always moving because we couldn't pay the rent. It got so that I didn't even try to make friends. What was the use, we were always moving? The only thing I had going for me was that I was good in sports and the kids accepted me for that. Things seemed to escalate at home. The more Dad drank the more violent he would get, sometimes throwing things at Mom or striking her. There were many bad scenes that have had a permanent effect on me. The next story was life changing and is forever imbedded in my memory.

CHAPTER 3

A life-changing experience

I was ten years old at the time and had just come home from school to find my mom lying on the floor all black and blue and my dad kicking her with his leather shoes on. Mom was crying and begging him to stop. I started pulling on my dad, telling him to stop. He just tossed me across the room and then picked my mom up and tossed her out into the snow. He then grabbed me by the shoulders and said, you have to decide who you want to live with me or your mom. I was sobbing and shaking and said I want my mom, so he tossed me out too. He followed by throwing out our jackets and Mom's purse. So, we left with nothing but the clothes on our backs. We walked to the bus stop which was half a block away, caught the bus and went across the city to our old neighbour Leona Murray whom was a good friend of Mom's when we lived next door to her. We knocked on the door and Leona answered, grabbing Mom, hugging her and asking what happened? Mom kept crying for her baby (Sylvia) who was only two at the time and was sleeping upstairs when everything happened. Dad wouldn't let her take Sylvia. Mom phoned her brother Ernie who lived in Outlook and he said that he would come and get us and take us out there.

Now I knew that I had to act fast because he would be here in two hours. Realizing that Leona and Mom would probably like to talk without having me within earshot, I asked if I could have a quarter to go get some candy at the store close by. Leona quickly obliged and I went on my way but instead of going to the store I used the money to take the bus back to Dad's, across town. I had never ridden the bus alone before so that was scary and I had to transfer buses at the Bay, but I made it. When I arrived there, my brothers were home from school but my Dad was nowhere to be seen. He had gone to the bar. That was his way of handling things. I knew he would never look after my little sister properly and I hated to think of what would happen to her. My brothers asked, "what are you doing here?"

I replied with, "I changed my mind I want to live with you guys." I asked where Sylvia was and was told she was sleeping upstairs. I went up and woke her and said let's go play with our pet bunny in the garage. I didn't want to cause suspicion so I didn't dress her too warm, just put her jacket on but no hat or mitts. Instead of going in the garage we went out to the alley and down the alley to the bus stop, caught the bus and headed back over to Leona's place. When Mom saw Sylvia, she just kept crying "my baby, my baby." What a reunion that was. My Uncle Ernie arrived soon after and took us out to Outlook.

When I say that the above was a life-changing experience, it is because that is when I turned against God, believing that there was no God, because if there were, He would never have let my mom whom I loved dearly, suffer like that. It had the same effect on my mom because the church wasn't there for her. When she went to the pastor previously, she was told, "You made your bed now you have to lie in it."

CHAPTER 4

A ray of sun before the cloud

My memories of Outlook are probably the happiest times of my childhood or at least for the most part. We got to stay at Grandpa's farm which was a mile north of Outlook. This was where I finally got to know my grandfather on Mom's side. He had never remarried after my grandma died in the pandemic. He and I planted a garden together and he taught me many things. I was in my element, with nature all around. I climbed trees to see the baby birds, I even tamed a pigeon. Whenever I went outside, I would whistle and the pigeon would fly down from the barn, land on my shoulder, and give me a kiss. Mom worked hard for Grandpa cooking cleaning, washing clothes, and running errands. It was a win-win situation for all of us. The family that lived in the farm across the road, was a well- respected family in the community and seemed like really nice people. My cousin Carmen said that they had a couple of horses and that we could probably ride them if we asked. I was all for it because I loved animals and I had never had the chance to ride a horse.

When we finally had the chance to go there, Carmen was the one asking because she knew him. Murray Cameron was very nice and so accommodating. He said we could only ride "Big Red" because the other horse was too spirited, so we had to ride double, but that was okay, we didn't care. He said we could ride any time we wanted to; I was ecstatic! One day however, when we were out riding, we heard Murray call to us, he was mending a fence and asked for our help. We road over there and he said MaryAnn will you come help me and Carmen will you go find the cows for me? I dismounted and trudged over to where he was. We were happy to feel useful since he was so nice to let us ride "Big Red." Once Carmen was out of site, I realized he didn't care about the fence, I was his main target. He pulled me deeper into the trees and started to kiss me and molest me. Now, I understand the expression when they say "the lamb was quiet before the slaughter." I absolutely froze in fear. I couldn't scream, I couldn't run, he could have done whatever he wanted to do to me that day; I was helpless.

Suddenly Carmen was calling, "MaryAnn, where are you, where are you," and I knew I had to alert her to where I was so I could get away. It scared Murray too, because he knew the jig was up. He straightened my clothes and let go of me.

I screamed, "Here I am! Here I am!" I ran for all I was worth to get to her and it took two tries to get up on the horse, I was shaking and crying as I said, "get out of here as fast as you can." We took the horse back to the barn and left as fast as we could.

Later when I got home, I told Mom what had happened. She said people probably wouldn't believe it because Murray was a well-respected family man with a wife and four daughters. She suggested I keep it to myself. I was hurt at this but in hind sight and knowing my mom like I did; she didn't want to cause trouble for Grandpa or Carmen's mom and dad. I think she took me seriously because it wasn't too long before we moved to Prince Albert to live with Mom's Aunty Haldis and her grown daughter. Mom's idea of dealing with it was to remove us from the problem.

CHAPTER 5

What now?

Aunty Haldis and her daughter were very nice in taking us in but it meant another change to adapt to. Another new school and more strange kids to relate to as well as new teachers and new surroundings. No wonder I was shy, it is so hard to fit in when everyone already has friends except for you. Mom struggled to support us because she could only get low paying minimum paying jobs. In the spring my brother Don came for a visit and he was begging Mom to come back to Dad. He said that Dad was changed and that things would be different, he promised. I think that because she felt so sorry for my brothers, she decided to give it one more try for their sakes.

The next move was back to Saskatoon where we moved into a two-story house and lived in the upstairs suite. It was very small but we were all together again. I was in grade seven and attended Westmount school which I liked very much. Before I knew it, they had me pitching on the senior baseball team which was made up of all grade eight kids and they even made me captain. I was popular because of the sports but very shy otherwise. I even got an invite to pitch for the

SaskTel Women's softball team. I was starting to come out of my shell but then my bubble was about to burst.

The old life was returning. Dad was drinking heavy and getting into it with Mom once again. This time Stu my eldest brother who was about eighteen at the time, got between them and Dad turned on him. Dad grabbed him around the neck and started choking him, he couldn't talk but as he was turning blue, he reached in his pocket and drew out a pistol which he put on my Dad's temple and Dad shockingly released his grip on Stu's neck. I guess Stu had come prepared because he could see how things were progressing between Mom and Dad and he knew that he had to do something. I don't know if the rent was not paid or what exactly happened, but suddenly we were into another move and another school. Now I was in grade eight at Caswell School. My grade eight was a total write off as I could not concentrate on school. I just kept watching the clock and I couldn't wait till four o clock to go home and see if my mom, whom I loved dearly, was dead on the floor. My brothers were starting to get lives of their own and had girl friends but they always told me where they were going and told me to phone them if there was trouble. One time when Dad was in one of his tyrants Don came to Mom's rescue. I know that he felt bad for coaxing Mom to come back when he saw that nothing had changed. He was only about sixteen and he was scared stiff of Dad but he got between them and told him to leave her alone or else. I remember Don shaking as a leaf as he said it. Dad swung around and tried to slug Don but Don was quicker and laid one on my dad which sent him into the mantle where he cracked his head open. That was the end of my mom and dad's life together.

Mom, sister Sylvia and I moved into a small basement suite and Dad and the boys moved to Regina where Dad started up Regina paving and the boys worked for him. Wasn't long till Stu got married and Don joined the army.

CHAPTER 6

Relief before the betrayal

Because my schooling went to pot in grade eight, I was passed conditionally. That meant that I had one month in grade nine to prove myself and if I couldn't then I would have to go back and repeat grade eight. With all the tension at home gone, I had no trouble improving my school work and passing grade nine. Grade ten was going great and once again my sports achievements were gaining me favour with the kids. Now it was basketball and track that I was excelling in. I was starting to see the light at the end of the tunnel but then the unthinkable happened.

My mom had been working at a convenience store and came home one day to tell me that she was going to marry her boss and we were going to live at his house. She proceeded to tell me that he was an alcoholic but that he wasn't violent, that he was very nice when sober and that he was harmless when he drank and he didn't drink in public because he was a business man and didn't want people to see him drunk. Alcohol had been the demon in her first marriage and I just couldn't see why she would even think of marrying another alcoholic but what did I know? I guess Mom had been so put down by my dad that she didn't have a very high opinion of herself and didn't think she deserved better.

So, we moved into Bill Hansen's three-story house. The second and third floors were rented out suites, we lived on the main floor. I had to move in with his daughter Janice who had a bedroom in the basement and sleep in her double bed with her. Now I had never met her before and I found her to be the most, foul-mouthed, partying, pardon the word, slut. She was 2 years older than me and totally opposite to me. I was interested in sports and had not even thought about boys yet. I hated every minute around her. The night before I was to go write my grade 11 exams, she was persistent that I go out with her boyfriend and his friend who was just travelling through Saskatoon because he was delivering a new car (Lincoln Mark11) from Calgary to somewhere down East. I felt ill at ease and didn't want to go but she insisted and said nothing would happen and she would get me back early. I reluctantly went and here I was really out of my comfort zone, totally naïve compared to them. They parked just outside of the city limits and broke out the beer. They were playing chug-a-lug and wanted me to play. Janice said, "Don't worry, I'll look after you and nothing will happen, I promise." Needless to say, I fell for it, trusted her and got drunk because I had never had a drink of alcohol before, it hit me very hard. That's exactly what they wanted. I was being set up. Luckily as they were driving back into town to go to Janice's boyfriend's place, they drove off the rode at a dead-end construction site and I was thrown into the windshield and ended up in the hospital with lacerations and a broken nose in five places. I think that accident saved my life, or at least from going down a very wrong path, for I later found out that Janice's boyfriend's friend had just gotten out of jail and that Janice's boyfriend was himself in and out of jail several times. I should have listened to my gut feeling in the first place. Hence, I never wrote my grade II exams but that was a small price to pay considering what may have happened.

Shortly after all this happened, Janice found out she was pregnant and her dad sent her away to have the baby and give it up for adoption, which she did and then she went to live with her mom down in the United States. I was ecstatic when she left. Now I had the bed to myself and the room to myself. Now life would be better, or would it???

I had just started to accept Bill Hansen as Mom's husband and decided that if he made her happy then that's all that mattered. For the first time in her life Mom finally had a piano. You see, she was a great pianist but never owned a piano or had one in the house, but after her dad passed away, Uncle Ernie asked if Mom wanted the old piano that her dad had given her mom when they got married. It was old but had a great sound. All of her siblings were piano players too, but they had pianos (newer ones) and didn't want the old piano. Bill Hansen played an alto sax and as a result, he and Mom made beautiful music together. It was so nice to see Mom in her element and with a smile on her face.

Bill Hansen was a prosperous business man and owned a confectionary, a barbershop and a beauty parlour all under one roof. He always said that you could make the best money barbering because you had the least overhead and inventory and you could put through many more patrons in one day at almost clear profit. Because of this, I decided to take a barbering course though the Saskatchewan Institute of Applied Science and Technology (SIAST). He said I could do my one-year practical in his shop and then write my exams to get my journeyman's ticket. He said that barbers made more money than hairdressers and I thought that he should certainly know as he had experience in both. Sounded like a good thing to me, so that's what I did later on in the story.

Looking back, I can see the ulterior motive he had in leading me into barbering. He had his eye on me for other things, which I was too dumb to realize at the time. When he was sober, he was no problem, but when he drank, especially when he was just starting into a binge, he would start making passes to me and asking for sex. Said he would buy me a car, etc., if I would co-operate. It just made me sick that he would say these things to me and I thought he was a scum bag. When he was in this stage, he would go up to his business place after hours go in and drink vanilla which he stole from the shelf in the confectionary or go into the barbershop where he drank the shaving lotions. When it got to the point that he couldn't drive anymore he would ask me (without a licence) to drive him to the bootleggers. You see, he didn't want any of his customers to see him in that state, so he would go to bootlegger's rather than a bar. Mom allowed it because she said he could never drive without maybe killing someone. She said that if I got caught driving without a licence, they would pay the fine. I got to know where all the bootleggers were in Saskatoon and when he was done, I would pile him into the car and take him home. When he was this far gone, I wasn't afraid of him because he could barely stand up. I could easily handle him. It was when he first started drinking that he was the most dangerous, as he was over six feet tall and could probably very easily overpower me. I was getting more and more scared of him. Through all of this, Mom knew nothing; she was working herself to the bone in his confectionary store and I just couldn't tell her what a pig she had married and what he was really like. Things would get worse...

I was down in my room getting ready to go out. I was putting on some makeup and had a bottle of foundation in my hand when he came in, and threw me on the bed and landed on top of me. He was trying to rape me but I still had the bottle of foundation in my hand and knowing how particular he was about his expensive suits I poured it all over the back of his suit. This made him jump up quickly and he said, "What am I going to tell your Mother?" I said, I don't care what you do, just leave me alone and get out of here. This was when I knew that I had to get out of that house at all costs before he actually did rape me. I even tried running away but after spending the night in a laundromat and under the Broadway Bridge, hungry and cold I went back home. Mom was totally distraught, but I couldn't tell her why I did what I did. I saw the hurt in her eyes and it nearly killed me. What could I do, I had no way of making a living for myself yet and had no place to go, so the only thing left for a girl to do in my generation was to get married? I vowed that the first man to ask me to marry him, I would whether I loved him or not. I had to get away from Bill Hansen.

CHAPTER 7

Big mistake

One day when I was about sixteen, Mom and Bill went away on a short trip and left me in charge of working the late shift at the confectionary, counting the cash, leaving a float for the next day and bringing the cash home by cab, as I still had no licence and no car. Being that it was a nice summer day I decided to walk up to the confectionary. It was about twelve blocks away but I was young so that wasn't a concern. After about four blocks, a car pulled up alongside of me and a balding man of about forty years old or so was asking for directions to get to the Mayfair Swimming Pool. He said he was a jewellery salesman from Regina and was just visiting in Saskatoon. He asked me where I was going and I told him. He asked if that was anywhere near the Mayfair Swimming Pool and I said yes it was and I tried to describe how to get there. He said, "Well maybe you could show me how to get there and I could drop you off at your work. Hop in." He seemed very genuine and he looked harmless so I got into his car.

Big mistake! Everything was going okay till he got to where he was to let me off (corner of Ave H and 33rd street). He slowed down and then all of a sudden sped up. That's when

I realized he had no thoughts of dropping me off but rather wanted to get me out of town—two blocks further and we would be at the outskirts of Saskatoon where I would be at his mercy and be raped and or maybe killed.

My instincts told me to get out of the car at all costs, so I opened the door and bailed out of the car while it was moving. I got banged-up and skinned-up but I was alive. He sped off as fast as he could go, probably fearful of being recognized or something. Amazingly, no one was a witness to any of this but I sure learned a hard lesson when I thought about how close I had come to disaster. I picked myself up and although hurting, made my way back the block to the confectionary. Thank heavens it was a busy night and the time went fast. I couldn't wait to get home and nurse my hurting body and tarnished ego. About half an hour before closing that same man came in and bought a package of cigarettes. He never said anything because there were other people in the store but I started shaking as soon as I saw him and I was thinking what if he comes back when I close. Thankfully there was a constant run of customers and I was never alone in the store. At closing time, I dealt with the last customers and then immediately locked the door and called a cab. I got the float ready for the next day, piled all the money in an inconspicuous money bag and waited for the cab. I made it home safely. Somehow I was spared again. Thank goodness he didn't have child locks (not invented yet) in his car for then I would never have been able to escape. I trusted a stranger and nearly paid for it with my life.

CHAPTER 8

Dating

My very first date was with a boy named Colin. He asked me to go to a drive-in with him and I said yes. He was super shy, just like me. You won't believe it but we both fell asleep as the movie was playing. We never kissed or held hands or anything. We were too shy to talk and the movie wasn't that great. We both woke up about 5 a.m. to find that we were the only car left on the lot. We were so embarrassed. He drove me home and we never saw each other again.

My second date was with a girlfriend's boyfriend's friend. I really liked Ed. We went steady for two weeks but then he broke up with me and I was heart broken because I thought that he would be my escape from Bill Hansen.

In July, while my cousin Carmen and I were at the Exhibition grounds, we met Mike Scherbluk who was a somewhat friend with my brothers. He was funny and care-free and made me laugh. I went out with him a few times after that and he was fun to be around. In August at my girlfriend's wedding, he proposed to me in the food line and I said yes. I knew that he had too much to drink but I still accepted because I was desperate to get out of home. I figured that in time I could learn to love him, after all, look at all the arranged marriages in other countries (with no love) that seem to work. Why wouldn't this one.

By the time we started planning our wedding, I feared that I might be pregnant. You see, in those days there was no such thing as birth control and I knew nothing about how to prevent a pregnancy. I was super naïve about everything. When I shared with Mom that I thought I might be pregnant and that Mike and I were going to get married, she was worried about what Bill Hansen would say and that he would probably want to send me away to have the baby and put it up for adoption like he had done with his daughter Janice. I immediately said that there was no way that I was giving up my baby. She suggested that we go ahead and get married quietly and she would let on that she knew nothing about it, so that's what we did.

We got married at St. Thomas Westley United Church on the 29ᵗʰ of September, 1962 with only my brother and his girlfriend standing up for us. I was 18 years old and Mike was 22 years old. There was no wedding dress, no wedding cake, no Mom or other family. I felt like such an outcast and a loser. While we were getting married, Mom and Bill Hansen were at Mom's cousin's daughter's wedding with all the pomp and ceremony usually accustomed to a wedding. I felt cheated and hurt that not even my mom could be at mine and that I had to let everyone think that we eloped. At least I was finally away from Bill Hansen.

CHAPTER 9

Married and a mother

Our first home was a basement suite which was very cold in winter. It was so cold that there was frost on the walls and the sheets stuck to the frost on the walls. We were very poor and could afford nothing else. Luckily in the spring we qualified for subsidized housing where the rent is according to your monthly income and we moved into Gladmer Park which was much nicer. We had neighbours on both sides and everyone had things in common. It was a good place to raise kids.

On April 9th, 1963, William Michael was born and we started a new life as parents. I was so in love with this dark-haired cutie-pie. He was so perfect in every way. I marvelled at being a mother and all that entailed. I would never be the same again. I remember leaving the hospital with my precious new baby and the nurse checking me out. It happened to be Easter and she said, "I'll see you next year."

Guess what? Next year with Easter being two weeks earlier, there I was again giving birth to another baby boy, Robert Thomas, perfect in every way. Now Bill would have a playmate. I was so happy. Bob turned out to be a super loving and affectionate baby who rarely cried.

With two new mouths to feed things were getting pretty tough financially. Mike was very unstable, couldn't seem to hold a job and was out of work more than he was in. We were two totally opposite people. As much as I tried to make things work, there was no security in our relationship. He never seemed to grow up. He wanted to be the man of the house and take care of rent and bills, but the bills and rent sometimes never got paid. I figured I could do better on my own.

I found a little tiny one-bedroom house on Second Street in the Nutana area of Saskatoon and moved in with the boys. I put the boys' two cribs in the bedroom, which was very small, and I slept on the couch. I was barbering at that time so I needed a babysitter to watch the boys. I got a woman who lived nearby. She seemed like she would be perfect for the job. Everything was going fine until I got a frantic call from her, while I was at work, saying that there had been an accident and that I better come home right away. I rushed home to find her holding 11-month-old Bob in her arms, with a gash on his upper eyelid and stuff from his eye hanging out. His eyeball was swollen up like a golf ball and he was listless. I asked her what happened and she said, "Bill pushed him and he fell on the floor." I had trouble believing that because the floor was linoleum. What could have caused the gash? I rushed him to City Hospital Emergency as fast as I could go.

In no time, there were four doctors looking at him and questioning what happened? I told them what the babysitter said and they said no way, something had penetrated deeply into the eye socket. They said to get him to the university hospital right away because he needed the specialists there. Out to the vehicle I went. I drove there holding Bob in my arms while driving a stick shift. Not sure how I did it but I did.

They took Bob from my arms and immediately another group of doctors surrounded him. The doctors kept asking what happened and when I told them, they didn't believe it. Then I asked if it could have been a foot-long nail file, because I had seen the babysitter using one and I told her to please not leave it on the coffee table where the boys could get it but rather put it up on the fridge or in her purse. The doctors agreed that it could have been that and that they would know better once they got inside. Later that night they did surgery and thank heavens the nail file, or whatever, hadn't penetrated the back of the eye and into the brain. He would be fine.

Bob's accident was the wake-up call for me and I realized that I needed help to raise the boys. Mike and I got back together and this time I vowed to myself that I would make it work no matter what!

We rented a small house in the Mayfair district and settled in once again to try and make a go of it. I really wanted to have a daughter (possibly two to complete what I thought was the perfect family of two boys and two girls just like my mom had) and Mike was of the same mind. It wasn't long till I was pregnant again. It's funny because there didn't seem to be any doubt in my mind that I would have a girl and sure enough, Kathy Ann was born. Well, you never saw a prouder Mom; I finally had my girl. Not that the boys weren't important, they sure were, but I think every mother would like to have a daughter just as every father would like to have a son.

I'll tell you a little story about what happened when I was pregnant with Kathy, and I would definitely not recommend it to anyone else. You see, I had such a craving for ice cream and bananas that I gained so much weight with her. It was summertime and very hot that year making it so uncomfortable to be carrying all that extra weight. It was a Friday: I had just come from the seeing the doctor and he said that if I didn't have the baby over the weekend, he would induce me. Now, I had heard all kinds of horror stories about other women who were induced and how painful it was. There was no way that I was going to let him do that to me, so I took matters into my own hands (not a very smart thing to do). I got a ladder and I climbed it to get on top of our picket fence. I held my swollen belly to not hurt the baby and then jumped off of the fence hoping that that would start labour. It worked because I went into labour shortly afterwards and Kathy was born on Sunday. A perfectly healthy 9-pound, 10-ounce baby girl. I shudder to think of what could have happened through my ignorance on the subject.

It was while we were living here, that we had our car repossessed. Once again Mike had not made the payments. He just never showed any responsibility and I wondered if he ever would.

We wanted to purchase a house but that seemed like an impossibility as we never had any money for a down payment. One day however, Mike came home and said he had been talking with a guy who wanted to sell his house. It would be a rent to own. That means you rent for one year and if all goes well, then that rent money would act as your down payment and you could buy the house. We jumped at it because that was the only way we would ever to be able to buy a house. The cost of the house was $11,500.00 and our rent for the first year was $100.00 a month and then payments there after were $100.00 per month.

The kids were one, three, and four when we moved into the house. It was situated right across the street from the Exhibition Grounds in Saskatoon. We were so happy to finally have a place to call our own. These were the best years of our marriage. We had great neighbours who were older than us and I looked up to them and learned a lot from them. They liked Mike because he was so happy-go-lucky and funny. We would get together often.

Kathy was three years old when we started to feel that she needed a playmate. Mike would say let's try for another girl. I said, "no way, I don't want to go through another year of washing diapers and hanging them out on the line, bring them in frozen and then finish drying them in the house." It was so hard on the hands. Secretly, I wanted to try for another girl too but thought I could use this to my advantage so I said, "if you get me a clothes dryer, I'll get pregnant again." Nine months later, Tracey was born and completed my dream of having what I thought was the perfect family of two boys and two girls. Tracey was born with a heart murmur, caused by a tiny hole in her heart, but by her one-year checkup the hole had grown in and all was well.

I absolutely adored my children. They all had their own personalities which made each one unique and beautiful. Life took on new meaning as now I had a purpose in life and a very important role as their mother. I would protect them at any cost.

CHAPTER 10

A lapse in time

Mike finally got a job out at Allan Potash mine as a painter and I was cutting hair on the side. Things had improved quite a bit in our relationship, if only he would stop embarrassing me in public. You never knew what he would blurt out that people would find offensive and off- colour. I guess he couldn't help it because that's what he grew up with. His mother was like that.

One day we were invited to a pool party by some neighbours in the next block. I wasn't feeling well and we didn't have a babysitter, so I didn't go. Mike decided that he would go down for a little while just to put in an appearance. Well it turned out to be a long while. I found out the next day that he had too much to drink and went skinny dipping in their pool. I was mortified to say the least. This was just one of many, many times that he did something to cause embarrassment and humiliation. He thought it was funny, to me it was anything but funny.

It was around about this time that my mom sold the quarter section of land that her dad had willed to her. She and Bill Hansen had tried farming it but then Bill had a heart attack and they decided to sell it. When Mike found out that Mom had some money, he said that he was going to talk to her and see if he could borrow $10,000.00 from her for a down payment on a small country hotel in Alvena, Saskatchewan. He said that he had always dreamt of owning a small country hotel. I was definitely not keen on the idea. I didn't think it was the proper place to be raising kids, especially when I heard that our living quarters would be right next to the bar. Mom lent him the money and the deal went through. Before we could take possession and get our liquor licence, we had to take a compulsory weekend Hotel Management course in Regina. Little did I know that this move out to Alvena would lead to the end of our marriage.

CHAPTER 11 - TURBULENCE

The hotel consisted of a long narrow bar: I think the seating capacity was thirty-two, if I remember correctly. Our living quarters were next to the bar and consisted of a very large kitchen and a dining room for anyone wanting a meal that was not in the bar setting. Sometimes the teachers would come and have a meeting with a meal. On the other side of the dining room was our bedroom. It was huge. We had two double beds in it, one for us and one for the girls. The boys shared one of the hotel rooms upstairs, and at the end of the hall was a bridle suite which was bigger and a little nicer.

I got the three oldest kids enrolled in school, which was basically out to the back alley and across the street which made it very handy. Tracey was only two at the time so we gave her toys to play with in the kitchen while we were busy. One of her favourite things was when we gave her records from the jute box, she would play them for hours on a little portable record player we gave her. I would be in and out of the kitchen as I filled orders for hamburgers, chips and/ or full meals as they were ordered from people in the bar.

Mike fit into the community quickly because he could speak Ukrainian and it was a Ukrainian settlement. They liked his jovial spirit and the fact that he would sit down and drink with them. I on the other hand always felt like an alien. It was a real drinking community where half of the people were Ukrainian and spoke Ukrainian and the other half were Cree from the One Arrow Reserve and spoke Cree. I could speak neither of these languages and felt uncomfortable when they were speaking their language because I never knew if they were talking about me.

I never worked so hard in all my life as I did out there. During our opening hours, I worked the bar, I cooked and cleaned, I rented out rooms and washed bedding, I even cut hair on the side. The trucks came early in the morning, delivering liquor and beer in cases and kegs. Trucks bringing pop, potato chips, bread, etc., and all that stuff had to be put away so there was lots of heavy lifting. For our groceries, one of us would have to go into Saskatoon every few days to the Cash and Carry wholesaler to get the stuff, while the other one manned the hotel. The bar was busy from 11 a.m. to 1 a.m. and then when it closed, I had to clean the bathrooms and the bar. Sometimes people had thrown-up in the bathroom; it was not nice. I did all this while Mike counted the cash and got the float ready for the next day. We were lucky if we could get to bed by 2:30 a.m. or 3:00 a.m. and then up again when the trucks started coming at 7:00 a.m. Looking back now, I don't know how I did it all.

Through this time, I could see the effect this was having on our kids and I didn't like it. We had no time for them and they were running wild with no supervision. Mike was drinking far too much, sitting with the customers and not tending to business. I too acquired a taste for draft beer because we couldn't drink the tap water as it was so hard and was a bright orange colour. I never drank to excess though. I didn't like what all this was doing to our family and I wished we had never moved to Alvena.

One evening on a very cold winter night, the bar was full as usual, and one of the patrons asked where Joe was. His jacket was on the chair but he wasn't and they said that he wasn't in the bathroom either. My heart just sank and I thought immediately about my girls. I ran through our living quarters to our bedroom and sure enough, Joe had my six-year-old daughter Kathy on her back with her nightie up to her neck. I was like a she-bear protecting her cubs, I was wild, I hollered and screamed at him and told him to get out of the hotel and never come back. I chased him through the lobby and out the door with no jacket, into a horribly cold winter night. I didn't care if he froze to death that night. All I could think of was him maybe hurting my daughter. What really made me mad was that when I told Mike what happened he didn't think it was a big deal. He said Joe probably wouldn't have done anything anyway. This is when I told him that I hated Alvena and I wished we had never come here. Later I found out that Joe had gone a half block down to the Co-op store and they had taken him in as they also had living quarters at the back of their store.

Another episode happened when Mom and Bill Hansen came out to spend a few days between Christmas and New Year's. We got invited to a New Year's party but we weren't going to go. Since we had never been anywhere except at the hotel, they urged us to go and they would look after the kids, etc. Everything was going well at the party and I was meeting some people other than patrons from the bar. Mike had been acting up (life of the party) but then I noticed he was missing. I asked where he had gone and was told that he went to get more booze from the hotel. I thought, Oh no! He had already had too much. Then there was a call, Mike asked for me, and told me that when he got home the hotel was on fire but he had gotten everyone out safely, except the dog had run back in. Some one from the party drove me home and I was just shaking in shock but so thankful that Mom and the kids were safe. They had all been sleeping when Mike aroused them and told them the place was on fire.

The firemen got the fire out quite fast and only the floor in the bar had burned through leaving a big hole. Most of the damage was in the basement storage area and one wall in the bar. They did find our pet dog overcome by smoke and laying on the girls' bed. Most of the damage was smoke damage.

Mike had later told me when we were alone that he started the fire and wanted to collect insurance so we could get out of the hotel business because he knew that I didn't like it. I never trusted Mike after that because I thought that if he could torch the building when his kids were sleeping in it then he was capable of anything. I told him that when school was done in June I was moving back to Saskatoon and he and his brother could run the hotel till we could sell it.

In the mean time we had a few helpers from the community help us wash down everything in the hotel. There was black soot everywhere and on everything. The Catholic church said that we could stay in the rectory till the hotel was repaired, etc. There were statues everywhere, even in the bedrooms. It felt so creepy to be there and the kids were scared of the statues but at least we had a place to stay till we could move back into the hotel.

Shortly after moving back to the hotel, there was a wedding in town and the bar was full of people killing time before the reception. Mike had been drinking all day and out of the blue he stood up in front of everyone and said that the drinks were on the house, help yourself to anything you want, "It's all on the house." And then he went into our living quarters and passed out on the couch. I had to be the bad guy and say that he didn't mean it, that he had had too much to drink. I gave them one free drink but said no to the cigarettes and other stuff.

I stayed true to my word and moved myself and the kids back to Saskatoon when school was finished in June. Mike got his brother Reg to come out and help him run the hotel. They ran the hotel all summer and then I got a call from Mike saying, "I'm out of here. I left the key in a special hiding place, it's your baby now." This is when Mom and Bill said to me, rather than you and the kids going out there again we will manage the hotel for you until it sells. One thing I knew for sure was that Bill Hansen was a good business man, my only worry was, could he stay sober? At this point he had been sober for about 5 years.

Things were going pretty good out there until Mom informed me that Bill was drinking and drinking a lot. I was so worried about Mom and how she was doing. It didn't take long however, and Bill was hospitalized and died. It was very quick. Now I had no other choice but to pull the kids out of school and move back out there, as there was no way that Mom could handle things alone.

I must say that Mom and I were a good team and worked well together. We soon had things running smoothly but I still worried about having the kids subjected to this environment and I was wishing with all my heart that someone would come, buy the hotel to get it off our hands and we could get out of this evil place.

It didn't take long for the news to get around that two women were running the hotel and that there were no men around. As a result, one night we awoke to find about eight indigenous people pounding on the door saying they wanted whisky. Mom went in to calm the girls should they awaken and I went to the door. I didn't dare open it for fear of what they might do, so I just hollered that we were closed and come back when we are open. They continued to bang on the door and then Mom said, someone was trying to come in the window in the kitchen. That's when I ran and got the 22-rifle put a shell into it and fled to the kitchen area. They already had the screen off and a guy was coming in head first. I was shaking but I hollered and pointed the rifle at his head and said, "You come one inch further and I'll blow your head off." I really meant it because I knew if they ever got in, my kids and my mother would be in danger. This was the second time my mother-bear instinct cut in and there was no way they were getting in even if it meant that I had to shoot him. By the way, Vonda was the closest R.C.M.P. detachment and that was half hour away. I was wild and I think they realized that I meant business because they backed off and left. I nailed the window shut and we went back to bed but sleep wouldn't come. We kept thinking what if they had gotten in.

Another time that we were tested to the limit was when I received a call from the Vonda detachment saying, "I know that it is just you and your mother running the hotel, but I have a predicament. We found on this stormy night a car broke down on the highway with two young men, an aunt and uncle, and two kids. We had to pick them up because they would have frozen to death. We have nowhere to house them. The hotel here won't take them because they are indigenous. We checked and they have money to pay for rooms, they seem very polite and appreciative and they promised me that they would be of no problem to you. Will you take them in? We will get them on their way tomorrow." We couldn't say no, especially when there were kids involved.

Shortly there after the R.C.M.P. arrived with our guests. I assigned the aunt and uncle with the two kids to the bridal suite upstairs and the two young men to two rooms next door.

After they got settled in, they came down to the bar. I asked where the kids were and they said they were sleeping. The officer was right in that they were all so well mannered and polite. We started to relax thinking that everything would be okay. Finally, the aunt and uncle went upstairs to go to bed but the two younger men continued drinking a bit longer and then went upstairs to bed. We were just shooing every one out at closing time and only had two guys left to get out (one was the principal of the school and the other a local farmer), when all of a sudden there was a lot of yelling and scuffling going on upstairs. The two guys in the bar, didn't want to get involved and exited the place. I locked the door and Mom and I went upstairs to see what was going on. The two young guys were fighting, they had broken a window, there was glass and blood everywhere. I hollered to Mom to go downstairs and phone the Vonda detachment. By this time the smaller guy was passed out but the bigger guy was still hitting him. I tried to get between them and get him to stop but he threw me to the side like a rag doll and I knew I better get out of there. I went downstairs to wait for the police. Mom and I were scared stiff. Suddenly it was quiet, not a sound coming from upstairs. All of a sudden, we heard sirens coming and lights flashing. We opened the front door to see six police cars screeching to a halt, and in they came with guns brandished. They asked, "Where are they?" We told them they were upstairs.

Vonda had asked for backup and that was why there was so many police cars. They were from Rosthern and Wakaw as well as Vonda. When they went upstairs both of the young guys were passed out on the floor. The aunt and uncle had locked themselves and the kids in their suite. They came out with heads down and just as scared as we had been. When we looked in the suite it was trashed. The kids weren't sleeping. They had gone into our basement storage area and stolen cases of pop and chips and bars. They had shaken the pop, opened it and sprayed it all over the room, they had crushed the chips all over the beds and floor, chocolate from the bars was everywhere. The room was a disaster. The police dragged the two guys out to their cars and took the aunt, uncle, and kids out to another car. Meanwhile they boarded up our broken window and apologized for putting us in this kind of situation. The next day, the Sergeant came back and put a new pane in our window and once again told us how sorry he was for putting us in such a perilous situation. He said that he should never have done that. He then told us that when he did a police check that morning, he found out that the big guy had just gotten out of prison in Alberta and was a really bad dude.

I was beginning to think that we might die here. I felt that this place was so evil. Our only hope was if the hotel sold; would it sell??? During this time Mike was working in northern Manitoba to get out of paying any child support. It was just Mom and I and I felt so bad having her and the kids suffer through this with me.

Finally, the hotel sold. We would be free. We could move back to Saskatoon and live a normal life. I was so happy when the deal was final and this chapter could close. After all the bills were paid, we only broke even—but we were free.

CHAPTER 12

What next?

The next nine months back in Saskatoon were really tough with four kids on my own and with no help from Mike. I had to resort to asking for welfare till I got on my feet. That was the hardest thing I had ever done. My pride was shattered, I felt like I was a real loser and a bad mother. I even contemplated suicide, but that thought didn't last because I couldn't bear to think of what would happen to my kids if I did that. I brought them into the world and I would look after them some how.

The barber shop that I had worked in was gone. I didn't know how I would make it on minimum wage. I was getting desperate. One day I saw an ad for a job at St. Paul's Hospital. I applied, went for an interview and was hired. I was simply ecstatic, as it paid more than minimum wage, it was full time and secure. I started to climb out of the pit of despair and see a glimmer of hope for the future.

It was around this time that Mom and I hatched a plan. She was going to buy a house and since the house on St Andrews was getting pretty small for the kids and I, we decided that if my place sold then I may have enough money to go halves with her on the down payment on a bigger house. Then she would be there when the kids came home from school and she wouldn't have to live alone. It would be a win-win situation for both of us. The kids loved the idea too. Luckily enough, our house sold quickly and I ended up with just enough money to go halfers with Mom on the house on Estey Drive.

We settled in there and everyone was happy. The kids loved having grandma there and their school was just across the back alley making things so handy. My oldest son Bill quickly became the man of the house, he cut the grass, did the barbequing and snow shovelling. He liked feeling important and needed. My son Bob helped out too at times. I could go to work feeling secure in the fact that my kids had someone to rely on when I wasn't there. This was a good time in my life and I have very fond memories of this time; but would it last?

CHAPTER 13

Dare to hope

One day. I can't even remember where or when; I met a man named John. He was taken by me and wanted to date me. My mind is fuzzy on all of this because I have tried for so many years to blot out all the bad stuff. I think that deep down I was looking for a father figure since my father was never there for me when I was growing up. I wanted a man to love me and look after me. John was fourteen years my senior but that didn't seem to matter. I had lived through so much and really felt older than I actually was. I guess I thought that maybe if I could find someone who loved my kids as well as me, that would be a dream come true. John made a big impression on Mom and he would be on the floor letting the girls comb his hair and put barrettes in it. He wined me and dined me and a year later asked me to marry him.

Mom decided she wanted to get a house of her own so John bought out her share and she got a house of her own about six or eight blocks away. After we were married, my eyes would be opened.

I never could have imagined the change in a person. Once the ring was on my finger, John was a different man. He was controlling to me and to my kids. All of a sudden, my son Bill couldn't touch the lawn mower or BBQ or anything else because John said he was the man of the house. My kids weren't allowed to have kids over or to use the phone. I was to come straight home from work and to tell him of my every move because he was jealous. We split all finances right down the middle and I was expected to buy all the groceries because I had the kids. He had one set of rules for his kids and a different set of rules for mine. Of course, his were favoured.

There was a dark cloud hanging over our house, the laughter and gaiety were gone. One day my son Bill came to me and said that he wanted to move to Edmonton to live with Mike. I was heartbroken to say the least but what could I do, he was old enough to make that choice and I knew he wasn't happy and wasn't being treated right here. When my son Bob heard that Bill was going, he wanted to go too, to be with Bill and Dad. Mike had told them how great it would be and the things they would do. Made it all sound so great. It was so hard to see them go but I felt like I was between a rock and a hard place. Years later, I would find out that John was pressuring them to go, telling them that they were too much of a burden for me and that they should be with their dad. If only I had known what was going on behind my back. Things got worse and worse. I had to do something. I told John I was leaving. I wanted to get as far away as possible and start a new life and never see him again. I didn't want to see my kids hurt anymore. Enough was enough. John gave me what I had put in for my share of the down payment for the house and the girls and I left. I found out later that he sold the house at quite a profit since Real Estate took quite a jump upward in value.

CHAPTER 14

Starting fresh

When I talked with Mom, I persuaded Mom to come with us. I had a younger sister out in Victoria and we could stay with her since she was living alone in a 3-bedroom duplex. I quit my job at the hospital and had 2 weeks vacation coming so it was my goal to get a job in that 2- week period so I wouldn't lose any income. We rented a U-Haul and off we went. We had spent 2 miserable years with John. Hopefully things would change, when we got far away from those hurtful memories.

We arrived and settled in. Sylvia put Mom in her bedroom which was upstairs and my girls in the room across from her. She took the bedroom in the basement and I slept on a cot near the furnace in the basement, which I didn't mind at all since I was always cold and felt the dampness of Victoria. The girls settled in quickly and soon loved Victoria. We had the nicest little lake at the end of our crescent. It was beautiful beyond words.

Job hunting began right away. Sylvia and I prepared a resume and out I went. People were saying that the job situation was pretty bleak because the economy had taken a downturn and people were getting laid off rather than hired. I knew that I had to find work, and fast. I tried all over the place and waited to hear back. On the very last day of my 2-week vacation pay period, I was hired at one of the hospitals, in the housekeeping department. I figured that if I took whatever job was available now, I could always try for other posting when they came available. At least I was working and would be able to support my girls.

About one month later I noticed a posting on the bulletin board for an O.R. Aide. I told my co- workers that I was going to apply for it. They laughed at me and said, "You'll never get it because you have no seniority." To their surprise I did get it. You see I had a lot of experience from working in St. Paul's Hospital in Saskatoon.

The girls settled into school and just loved everything about Victoria. They made friends and were happy again. It was nice for Mom to have her two daughters and two grandchildren all in one place.

One Sunday morning, Mom said that she was going to go to the little Baptist church at the end of the block and did we want to go along with her. I said, "No way, absolutely not." When she got back, she was raving about the nice people she met and that the pastor and his wife were so nice too. Next week, same thing, I said no again and she asked if she could take the girls with her. I said okay but don't ask me to go. A couple of days later she said she had invited the pastor over to meet with Sylvia and I. We felt like we were railroaded into this visit but reluctantly met with him anyway. He was a very nice man and he meant well when he invited us to come to his home. He said that he and his wife hosted a singles group at their home and we were invited to come if we wanted to. Sylvia and I went one night just to check it out. We were both surprised at what we saw and heard. These people had all kinds of stories, made my life not seem too bad, but I just didn't believe there was a God. How could there be when, as I said before, Mom was treated the way she was by my dad. Why, if there was a God, did he let that happen? If that was God, I wanted no part of it. The next Sunday came and Mom asked again. She said the girls were loving going to church and why don't I come too. I was just about to say no and then I saw the hurt in her eyes and I said, "Okay, just this once." While there I heard the gospel message but it didn't melt my cold, cold heart. I came home the same as before.

One night, I got a call from my son Bill asking if he could come live with me. I said by all means you can. He said things weren't going to well and he wanted to come home. When he arrived, I gave him the cot by the furnace and I moved a hide-a-bed into the attached garage and made that my bedroom. The garage door never closed all the way and there was about a four-inch gap at the bottom so I got visited by critters sometimes in the night. It was a good thing it never got too cold because the garage wasn't heated but I had lots of blankets.

CHAPTER 15

Understanding at last

One night at exactly midnight I awoke to a bright light in the room and soon realized it was the presence of the living God. Wow! He was there with me in that garage that I called my bedroom. Shakingly I got out of bed and fell to my knees on that oil-stained cement floor. Twenty-five years of tears flowed forth as I begged for forgiveness, for the mess I had made of my life. I asked Jesus to come into my life. It felt like a very heavy load had been lifted off of my shoulders. Somehow He made me understand what I couldn't understand before and I realized that He had been with me all my life, guiding me and protecting me. I didn't see Him, but I didn't have to for I felt His presence all around me. My life was changed that night and I have never been the same since. I prayed and poured my heart out to God for four hours, and then I opened the garage door and went for a walk down to the lake. Everything was different now. The grass was greener. I saw things that I never saw before. I saw God's handy-work in every leaf and tree and twig. I marvelled at how the birds sang and the water rippled. I had never noticed these things before. For twenty-five years I was just existing and trying to survive. Now life took on new meaning. I was loved by the creator of the universe. How could that be? But it most assuredly was. I was thirty-five years old but it felt like I was experiencing life for the very first time. The world and everything in it were beautiful, and for once I was at peace.

Now I wanted to go to church and couldn't get enough of it. Mom and the kids were happier. I could see the change in Mom, and it wouldn't be long before she gave her heart to the Lord and was baptized while in Victoria.

Soon I received a call from John, saying how much he missed us and would we consider coming back to Saskatoon and giving our marriage another try. He promised that things would be different. He said that he had changed. He said that Bill could live with us till he got a job and could make it on his own. What should I do now?

Since my conversion I had been reading the Bible every chance I got and now it seemed that I had to stay with my husband and that divorce was out of the question. That would be okay if he had truly changed but what if he hadn't and was just saying that to get me back? I should have gone to the pastor and explained things and gotten some advice but I didn't. I was trying to do things on my own again and not wanting to bother people with my problems. I finally figured that I had to go with the Bible, the word of God.

I gave notice at work and two weeks later John rented a U-Haul and came out to get us. The girls loved Victoria, their school and the friends they had made, so were understandably upset with the news. Bill had his doubts but said it was okay by him. He was sixteen and he had his own car, so he would follow in his car. By the time we got to Banff, I knew that it was a big mistake to think that John had changed or that anything would be different. It was here that he said Bill would have to get a place of his own and couldn't live with us.

I was devastated. How could this be happening again. I can't even imagine how my son Bill felt. He was a teenager trying to find his way in life and this was the ultimate rejection once again by a man that had no use for him and strived to keep him away from his family, the very ones who loved him the most.

Shortly thereafter Bill went back to Victoria. Mom and my sister had bought a house together and he could live with them and work with my sister's boyfriend who was a roofer. It was here that he met his future wife, Colleen, who lived next door. It was love at first sight and they would eventually marry, have three kids and spend twenty-seven years of happily married life until Bill died of a heart attack in 2011. We were all shocked by this news for he was only forty-eight-years old and, as far as anyone knew, he was in great health.

CHAPTER 16

Return to hell

When we got to Saskatoon, we lived in a new mobile home that John had purchased after he sold the home that Mom and I had originally bought. I got my job back at St. Paul's Hospital, and life returned to the abnormal normal that we had before. The difference was that now I was a Christian. I joined Emmanuel Baptist Church and was baptised. When my son Bob came from Edmonton for a visit John said that he couldn't stay at our place so he slept in his car. How could this be happening? John lied about everything. Then I found out that John was working on Kathy to get her to move out. He was always making fun of her and putting her down. That's really hard on a teenager who was in grade ten at the time. I knew then that he wanted all my kids gone, so he could have me with no strings attached. One day we had an argument and he said, "You have to decide between me or your kids." When he said that, there was no hesitation, I just said ok I will take my kids and go, and that's exactly what I did.

Children make themselves known by their deeds and their actions. I was too busy trying to keep peace to see their needs.

I should have been building self-esteem and confidence in my children, for they were looking to me to help them know how to believe in themselves, but I didn't believe in myself. I felt like such a failure. How could I give what I didn't have myself?

I am so sorry for what I put my children through during this failed marriage with John. I felt like I was between a rock and a hard place, trapped in a marriage that was no good for me or my kids. My dream of having a perfect life with someone who loved me and my children was shattered.

CHAPTER 17

Freedom

The girls and I moved into a duplex and started our new life together. We didn't have much but we had each other. The cloud had lifted and we could see new hope for the future. I got very involved in the church and Kathy got a part time job after school at an ice cream parlour down the street. Both girls had excellent marks in school and I was so proud of them. Life was much better now.

It was around about this time that my mom married Ed Marken. They apparently had known each other when they were seventeen and nineteen years old. Ed had asked my mom to go out with him several times but her dad wouldn't let her go. He needed her to cook for the thrashing crew. Mom was in grade eleven and Ed was already teaching at the College (LCBI) in Outlook, Saskatchewan. Things just didn't work out with Mom so Ed started dating another girl and eventually married her. Mom eventually moved to Saskatoon and got a job cooking for professors at the university in Saskatoon, and later met my dad and married him. Apparently, Ed's wife had died and when he heard that Mom was alone also, he decided to phone her in Victoria. They had not seen each other in fifty years so they immediately sent a picture of themselves to each other, wrote letters and planned their marriage over the phone. Then without seeing each other in person, Ed flew out to Victoria and they were married the next day. I think that they should have been married all along because they were perfect for each other.

When I first became a Christian, my very first prayer was for my mother. I prayed that God would give her a good life for the rest of the time she had on this earth. She had such a hard life and deserved to have some happiness and peace of mind. Little did I know, that God would answer my prayer way beyond what I could have ever imagined.

Mom and Ed were married in Victoria and then settled in Camrose, Alberta where he had been living at the time. They were sixty-eight and seventy-years-old when they got married and I thought that if they had ten good years together that would be great. They ended up having twenty years of a wonderful life. I was so happy for them and so glad to see my mom finally happy and content. God is so good and when He plans something, it's always the best, because he knows what's best for all of us.

CHAPTER 18

Life goes on

One day at church, a lady came up to me and asked if I would come in with her to start a Singles Ministry at our church. She said that there were about eight of us that never felt like we fit in. Some were divorced like myself and others were single for whatever reason, perhaps they never married or their spouse had died. I said sure and we started meeting at the church every Friday night. We tried to get a speaker in once in a while, we sang and had worship time. Once in a while we had a potluck supper and got to know each other's families. It really helped all of us feel more accepted at our church.

Soon we had a new comer to our singles group. He was a pastor who had been excommunicated from the Church of God Church that he pastored. Apparently, he had an affair with one of his flock and the church had kicked him out and his wife divorced him. He said that he went the way of the world, night clubbing, drinking and womanizing but had attended a church in Winnipeg where he was so moved at one of the services and went forward, leaving his wicked ways and turning back to God. He was in tears as he spoke of this.

What could we do but give him a chance as God forgave us, we should forgive him, shouldn't we?

Soon Paul became a very major part of the Singles Ministry at our church and the Singles Ministry grew from 8 to 150 in a very short time. There were singles coming from many different churches. Paul led the meetings and led the singing. He was able to get many really good speakers. There were many giving their testimony which in turn gave hope to those that had given up all hope. The church however was still very skeptical of him, wondering, if he had really changed. The lead pastor mentioned this one day, and I said, "Do you think that's fair? Look at all the people he has helped. Who are we to judge?"

Since Paul didn't have an office at church to counsel people, he met everyone in public, in coffee shops or the like. He sang in the choir, said all the right things, and showed every appearance of being a changed man. Finally, they even let him preach the odd Sunday morning service.

Almost right away he had his eye on me and was very nice to me. I met him for coffee every few days. We went to church and then out for lunch with a group of singles and Saturday evening he usually took me out for supper. This was how I lived my life for about nine years. Anytime the subject of marriage came up, he said he wasn't marriage material.

When I met him, I was living in a condo right around the corner from the church and he asked me if I wanted to move into one of his suites in his huge apartment block not far away. He said he needed someone to vacuum the hallways and clean the laundry rooms. He would deduct $100.00 off the rent if I did that and I could rent out my condo. It sounded good, and I could use a little extra cash anyway, so that's what I did.

The apartment block was huge so it was a little more than I had imagined, but it filled my spare time. Paul travelled quite a bit and when he was gone, he would leave me in charge of things in the apartment block. One time I had to call the city in to see where a terrible stench was coming from. They checked everything but couldn't find the source. After they left, I noticed that one of the suites on the bottom level had papers piling up under the door and out into the hall. I could hear the T.V. on inside. I knocked and knocked at the door but no one answered so I decided to use my master key and go in. I certainly, didn't expect to see what I saw. There was just the light from the T.V. and being that it was just before Halloween I thought someone was playing a joke. When I got closer however I could see that it was no joke. The young guy who lived in that suite had taken a shotgun and committed suicide. He was sitting on the couch with the gun between his legs pointing up to his head and the whole front of his head was gone. I was instantly shaking so bad that I was frozen there. I often spoke to this guy in the mornings when we would start our cars and then come back into the entranceway to stay warm till our cars had melted the frost off of the windows so we could see to go to work. He was a nice young guy in his early thirties. He had been dead for a while, hence the smell that everyone was complaining about. I wondered what had happened in his life to make him resort to this. What a waste of a young life.

My job at the hospital was going well and I was well respected there. I was teaching Pioneer Girls at church and of course heavily into the Singles Ministry. There were always things to do at the apartment block too. I was very busy to say the least.

When Tracey, my youngest child, graduated grade twelve and moved to Edmonton to take a course to become an Xray Technician, I really felt alone. I remember thinking, is this all there is to life? You get married, have kids, the kids grow up and then your job is done and the rest is just old age and death. There has to be more to life than that. I prayed to God to use me however He saw fit for the furthering of His Kingdom here on earth. I would go anywhere and do anything that He wanted me to do.

CHAPTER 19

Answering a call

Funny thing, it was only a few days later that I saw a video about Mercy Ships International, and the work that they do saving lives, bringing hope and healing to those less fortunate all over the world. At the end there was a call to come and be a part of Mercy Ships. I was so moved by what I saw; and I prayed asking God if this was where he wanted me to go. The more I prayed the more God impressed on me that that was where He was calling me. I filled out an application and then I waited. Afterall, that was the first step to going. If I wasn't accepted, that would be the end of it.

Before long I received a letter back stating that I had been accepted. Now here's where the rubber meets the road, would I answer the call? Fear suddenly came over me because I was afraid of the ocean and I got car sick just travelling across town in a bus. Why was God calling me to Mercy Ships, it just didn't make sense, or did it? After much prayer I realized that if God wanted me there, He would take care of all those things and I just had to trust Him.

Shortly after my decision to go, Satan tried entering into my life to foul things up. I got word that my oldest brother had committed suicide. I think Satan thought that would unnerve me and make me change my mind. It only made me more determined to do what God wanted.

I went to my boss at the hospital and asked for a one-year leave of absence and since I was working for a Catholic Hospital with a mission statement, I felt quite sure that I would get it, but no way. She said, "there is no way that I can let you go at this time. We are building a new wing onto the hospital and I need you. If you went next year that would be different." I said okay then, I'm giving my 2 weeks notice and going anyway. I also gave Paul notice at the apartment block. Now I was definitely committed, I did however ask God for a sign that I was doing the right thing and that it was His will, not mine.

The next day when I came out of the store after buying a few groceries, I found a note on my windshield. It read, "If you want to sell your car, phone me at blah, blah, blah." The ironic part about this is that I hadn't told anyone that I was thinking of selling my car. This was confirmation from God, I'm sure of it.

I wanted my kids to be ok with me doing this so I wrote or phoned each one telling of what I was going to do and asking for their approval. They all got back to me saying yes Mom go, we'll miss you but we'll be okay. The hardest thing was the fact that I was a grandma for the first time and a year is a long time to be away from a little one.

One of my friends had said that I could store my furniture in her basement since it was empty anyway. She and another friend committed to paying my board and room of $150.00 a month on the ship. I was all set to go, everything was in order. All I knew was that I would fly down to Wilmington, North Carolina where someone from my ship, the Anastasis, would pick me up.

There was a small group that saw me off at the airport. It was such a funny feeling. I didn't have one key on me; no house key, no car key, no place to call home. I was stepping out into the unknown all by myself. I would know no one when I got there but I knew that God was with me and He had my back.

It was pretty scary landing in Wilmington. The wind was blowing so hard making it hard to stay on your feet. A young blonde guy came up to me and asked if I was MaryAnn Mclean. He introduced himself and said he was from the ship and was supposed to pick me up. He loaded my things into his van and off we went.

CHAPTER 20

The Ship

When we got to the ship, I was so surprised by how big it actually was. We went onboard, I was shown to my cabin and then taken on an orientation tour. I would be sharing the cabin with a girl from the Broncs, with a heavy Brooklyn accent. She would be one of many roommates that I would have while I was on the ship. I immediately felt at home with all these people; they were my brothers and sisters in Christ.

The very next day I started my D.T.S. (Discipleship Training School) onboard the ship. We were a class of about thirty people from all over the world. I was one of only three Canadians. The other countries represented were France, Sweden, Switzerland, Germany, Africa, Bolivia, England, New Zealand and the U.S.A. We all had one thing in common and that was that we loved the Lord and wanted to serve Him. Being that we came from different cultures and different churches our D.T.S. classes would get us all on the same page as far as how we would care for and minister to the lost. We would be in classes till 4 p.m. and then we would do various jobs on the ship in our spare time. Because of my hospital background I was given the job of cataloguing medical and surgical supplies that would be used in the next outreach to a third-world country.

While in the States, we sailed all around the Eastern and Southern States, stopping in ports to pick up outdated medical and surgical supplies donated from hospitals and conducting tours of the ship, inviting doctors and nurses to come aboard to see what Mercy Ships is all about. We were able to recruit many for short term missions and some much longer.

There were many families working as crew, some had been involved since the very start up of Mercy Ships. In some cases, the only life their kids had known was life onboard the ship. There was a wonderful school onboard that taught from the New Zealand curriculum, which was one of the best in the world at that time. Where else could a child get a great education and all the while seeing the world. There was a church, bank, store, library, post office, beauty salon, and laundromat. The ship usually had about 450 people onboard at one time. We had quite the community.

We had our D.T.S. grad ceremony while the ship was in drydock for two weeks in Veracruz, Mexico. Once a year, the ship had to be taken right out of the water to inspect the part under the waterline, remove barnacles, repair as necessary and paint. While this was being done, we were put up in a hotel, from there we attended an international youth conference and did other outreach ministries. Once the ship was ready, we moved back onboard and settled in for our sail to the Dominican Republic.

It was interesting that in all the time that I was on the ship, I never once got seasick and believe me, we were in some pretty rough seas at times. I'm sure that was God's work. The thing I liked the most when we were sailing was watching the flying fish and the dolphins. It was like they were playing a game with us, following along side of the ship, jumping out of the water and then back in again. They would follow us for long periods of time. One time when we were far out at sea, no land insight, I was up on deck and noticed a colourful bird flying right beside the railing. It was going the exact same speed as the ship, so it was exactly even with me, I could have reached out and picked it out of the air. It looked so tired and worn out from flying. I thought to myself, he will either fall into the ocean and drown or if he has the nerve he will land on the ship, depending on if he trusted me not to hurt him. I think he may have gotten blown off track during his migration and was so tired that he just couldn't go on any longer. No sooner had I thought this and he landed on deck. I guess he figured he'd take a chance. Poor thing, he was panting and so out of breath. He just sat there for the longest time. I went and got a small container of fresh water and some bread crumbs and soon he hopped over to give it a try. Didn't take long after that, when he was rested up, he flew away. I sure hope he made it the rest of the way to wherever he was going.

When we arrived in Barahona in the Dominican Republic there was a large crowd of people at the dock to welcome us. News had travelled fast and people were curious as to what Mercy Ships was all about. Once we were moored things started happening quickly. Clinics were set up to assess people for surgeries, of course the worst cases were given priority. All of the operating rooms were putting through as many people as possible each day. Some people had to come as far as 30 miles on foot in the hopes of getting a life-changing surgery for free. Some carried a child or a loved one because they couldn't walk. Many had to be turned away because we never could have gotten to them all. Some would have to wait till the next time the ship came to their country.

I was trained to be a dental assistant and I worked with a dentist from New Zealand. Our team would leave the ship in the morning and go out to small villages where we would set up a clinic. People would come to have their teeth fixed at no cost. Some of those mouths had never seen a dentist before and were in terrible shape. My job was to suction patients and mix fillings for the dentist. One patient that left a lasting impression on me was a thirteen-year-old girl who had incisor teeth that hung out of her mouth giving her a Dracula appearance. She was afraid to be seen in public because she looked so ugly. The dentist pulled both of those teeth and she looked just beautiful, no need to hide away in shame anymore. While people were in the waiting room, we had the "Jesus" video going, in Spanish.

It was during my time on the Anastasis that the Bible really came alive to me. I saw the blind come on the ship not seeing, and then go off the ship with their sight, some for the first time in their life. One such man, 60 years old, was born blind and because he was poor and had no access to health care, was blind until our doctors removed his cataracts and gave him his sight for the very first time in his life. You never saw such a happy man.

Another case was a small baby who was sleeping in a plastic crib. There was a fire. The baby lived but one ear had been burned off. One arm because he had no access to health care had fused and healed to his side. The surgeons released his arm from his side, so now he could use it. They grafted an ear on and did other skin grafting to this cute little boy. He would have a follow-up surgery for more grafting the next time the ship came back.

A man with no arms came on the ship and was given prosthesis so he could feed himself for the very first time.

It gave him independence that he had never known before and he was so happy.

Many came on the ship crippled, not able to walk and went off the ship walking on their own.

Others had large tumours which deformed their looks and if left unattended, they would die a horrible death by suffocation. Mercy Ships gave them new hope and a future.

Other ways that Mercy Ships helped the community was to build houses, etc. Our cargo hold was full of supplies to do this.

We also held street ministries with puppets, songs, and a sermon message. Through the aid of an interpreter many people came to the Lord and then we passed them on to a local pastor who would work with them once the ship was gone.

I was also a part of a prison ministry. Before we ever went into the prison, we did a prayer walk around it, praying that we would be accepted by the guards and prisoners, and that Satan would not have any power there. When we got inside there was a main courtyard with buildings all around. On the roof there were snipers with rifles pointed at us and at the prisoners that were being let out into the courtyard. There was a small boy about two years old wandering around the courtyard and he was naked and looked so forlorn. I later found out that if a woman went to jail her kids went too. There were pigs and goats wandering in the courtyard also. The atmosphere was very oppressive with the prisoners yelling out obscenities. I was glad that I didn't understand Spanish.

We knelt in prayer and then continued with doing our skits, a sermon message, and a testimony from one of our team. After a few days of this, everyone relaxed including the guards. There was no reason for them to be on top of the rooves with guns displayed. Now they formed a fence around us with Billy clubs in hand, so much less threatening. The head of the prison said that he was happy that we were there, for the prisoners had all calmed down and were so much easier to handle. Many people came to the Lord and their whole demeanour changed.

When we noticed that a fourteen-year-old girl had recently given birth to a baby while in prison and the baby had no clothes, no blankets, nothing to wrap the baby in. Upon further inspection we were given the okay to take the baby to the ship because its umbilical was infected and without help the baby might die. You see, the young girl gave birth all by herself in her cell and had nothing to tie the umbilical cord except a dirty mop string she found on the floor. Which caused the infection. Later when they returned the healed baby back to her, the baby had clothes, blankets and everything a small baby would need. That young girl was so appreciative.

Karen, another person, and I from the ship were also given a part in teaching a Sunday School class to some of the prisoners. By now, they were so receptive to anything we had to say. They were in prison sometimes for such minor things. One had stolen a pair of shoes because he figured that if he had shoes, he would be able to get a job and be able to support his family. He had been arrested two years ago and his case had still not come to trial. Another fellow only had one ear. He said another man had cut it off with a machete when he was in a fight with him.

One time our ministry team was called by a pastor to come up to his church in the mountains near the border with Haiti. We accepted and went. It was quite a way to go and the roads were terrible but we made it. Because there were so many people, they never would have fit into the church so we held the service outside in the street. Everything was going fine until there was a great commotion, people yelling and now rocks being thrown. There was a group of Haitians that didn't want us there, they were into voodoo and the occult and found us to be threatening. The pastor's wife had been hit with a stone and blood was running down her face. There were several others in the same way. Our leaders from the ship piled all those that were hurt into our vans and took them to the ship to get stitched up. Meanwhile the pastor told us to take cover in the church till the vans came back to get us. The church was made of wood but you could see through the slats. The door was locked by a 4"x 4" board held in place by two brackets. By this time, it was getting dark and the Haitians had torches that they lit to see in the dark. I couldn't help thinking, I wonder if I will get out of this alive. We were all terrified because we knew that if they threw one of those torches on the roof of the church we were done, the place would go up like a match box. Immediately we were all kneeling on the floor praying like we had never prayed before. God answered our prayers for soon, we could sense that the group outside had quietened down and things were deescalating. We did make it back to the ship that night and once more we had seen God in action.

For part of our time in the Dominican Republic we stayed in a compound and worked out of there. When we first arrived, we were housed several to a room and one of the girls was first to take her stuff into a room. Suddenly we heard a scream and ran to see what was the matter. On her bed was the biggest frog that I have ever seen, it was the size of a tea kettle and I'm not exaggerating. Another time it was a snake crossing across the floor. At night we all had mosquito netting tucked in all around our bunk beds and that was to protect against the tarantula spiders. If you woke up in the night and shone a flashlight on your netting, there they would be. When we were at the compound we had to learn how to shower, wash your hair and brush your teeth with only one litre of water as fresh, clean water was pretty scarce. At first, I thought that would be impossible but later I mastered it and managed quite well.

After we were done our D.T.S. course and our outreach phase we were then given the opportunity to go home or to sign on for an extra three months as an associated crew member. Many of our class decided to go home but I chose to sign on for the extra three months to see what it would be like as a crew member. There was talk going around that the next outreach would be in Africa and that the ship would not be back to North America for a few years. This news wasn't what I wanted to hear because when we signed on to Mercy Ships, we had to make sure that we had fare to get home when our time was completed. At the time I signed up they said that would be from anywhere in the U.S.A. or Canada. If I was on the ship when it went to Africa, then I would have to be able to pay my fare home from Africa which I knew I couldn't do. The only other way would have been to raise support from other people and that just wasn't in my make up. That seemed to me to be like begging and something I just couldn't do, but I could pray.

On our way back to the States I prayed and prayed about it. It certainly was different now that I was an associated crew member. I was sharing a cabin with a black girl from Jamaica named Ebony and she had been on the ship for ten years. She was a great person whom years later I would meet in Red Deer at a Gospel Jamboree. I was given the job of being the head hostess, taking care of the VIP cabins and being the welcoming committee, I had two girls that had to answer to me and I had to wear a uniform. The V.I.P.'s were people coming from all over the world, some to see what Mercy Ships was all about, and some were coming as speakers in the next

D.T.S class. Some were reps from other countries wanting to see for themselves what we did and how we did it. It was very interesting, that's for sure.

On our way sailing back to the States, when we were sailing by Montego Bay in Jamaica, we were suddenly blasted with a siren. The captain told us to go to our muster stations for a head count, as they feared someone had fallen overboard. Now it is no easy task with a big ship like that, but we made a turn and headed back. As it turns out everyone was accounted for and it was later told to us that two boys with very active imaginations had sounded the alarm when in fact, it was probably just a dolphin that they saw.

CHAPTER 21 - PROPOSAL

Later when we were docked in Houston, Texas, Paul came for a visit and I was so surprised to see him. This is when he blew me out of the water when he asked me to marry him. He wanted us to get married and to lead the Senior's Ministry at our church back home. Secretly this was what I had wanted all along when I was back home. I wanted to be married and be in ministry together but he always said that he wasn't marriage material. Now I was confused. Why now? What does God want me to do? Maybe this was why I didn't have a heart for Africa because God was lining this up for us. I said I would pray about it and let him know before he had to leave Houston. The more that I thought about it and prayed about it, the more it seemed like the right thing to do. Paul had won over the senior pastor at our church and he was in favour of Paul having a more visible role in the church. I wanted it to be God's decision not mine.

Just before Paul headed to the airport, I said yes. I told him that I still had my three months to put in as an associated crew member, which should bring me home just before Christmas. We planned to get married on January 1st. Our senior pastor was going to marry us. Paul wanted to honeymoon in Hawaii for eight weeks before we would settle into ministry at the church. It all sounded like a dream come true. But would it be???

CHAPTER 22

Home again

I was so glad to be home and reconnect with my kids. It seemed like I had been gone for years and years. Before I had left, I put them all into God's care, praying that he would guard over them while I was away, and He did. I was so proud of them. Of course, Amanda, my first grandchild had grown like crazy while I was away.

Christmas came and went and then it was our wedding time. Our senior pastor married us in a very small intimate ceremony and then off we went to Hawaii for our honeymoon. It was supposed to be a wonderful experience, full of love and devotion to one another, but there was something wrong and I couldn't understand what it was.

CHAPTER 23

Broken dreams

We landed in Hawaii and arrived at our hotel, got unpacked and then went for a walk to see the sights. Something was bothering Paul; he wasn't acting normal. When I asked what was wrong, he said, "nothing."

The next day, he changed our hotel room to one with two beds. I was devastated. What had I done? Why was he treating me like a sister rather than a wife? Every afternoon from here on until we left Hawaii, he would disappear from 2 p.m. to 4 p.m. saying that he had to go be with the Lord in Prayer. We slept in separate beds and our eight-week honeymoon changed to a six- week honeymoon.

One time when we were at the north end of the island where the waves are really rough, he called me to the edge of the cliff to see the turbulent waters and I remember thinking to myself that no person could ever survive in there no matter how good a swimmer they were. Then all of a sudden, I had a foreboding feeling that I was in danger and something told me to step back out of the way. Paul had been standing behind me. Was he trying to get up the nerve to push me in there? I don't know, but you can probably answer that when you read further on, what happens when we get home to Saskatoon.

When we got back home, he said, "You can take the master bedroom and I will move to the spare bedroom." Then he dropped a bombshell and said that we weren't going to do the Senior's Ministry at the church but that he would be doing a prison ministry at the prison. He said he would be using Lorna, the piano player from the Single's Ministry. She could play and he would lead the singing as well as do the sermon message. What was happening? My dreams were crashing down all around and I had no explanation as to why??? I began to wonder if I was going crazy. This wasn't how it was supposed to be. Was there something wrong with me?

As time went on things did not improve and I was starting to think that perhaps there was something going on between Paul and Lorna. If not, then I was crazy and heading for a mental breakdown. I questioned why he was picking her up when they went to the prison. She had a car, so why didn't she drive herself? He said, "okay, okay I won't pick her up anymore." Somehow I didn't believe him and I had to find out if he was lying to me. After he left, I took a pair of binoculars and went out to the prison and hid in the tall grass and watched from a distance. Sure enough, there they came. He stopped the car then ran around to the passenger side and opened the door for her to get out. Then he popped the trunk and took out her keyboard and then they proceeded into the prison. After this episode, I had to find out what else was going on between them and decided to do a little more detective work.

I decided to get a small hand-held tape recorder, put it on top of the bookcase in his office. It would be voice activated so would only tape when someone was talking. Maybe that would incriminate him in some way. I was filling in for the church secretary at the time because she took a two-month leave, and I always left the home by 8:45 a.m. That night after Paul went to prison ministry I listened to the tape and sure enough, he was in a steamy sexual relationship with Lorna and had been for years and years. Lorna was the age of his oldest daughter and she was Mom to four young kids. Apparently when I was on the ship they had broken up and that was when he flew to Houston and asked me to marry him. When we were in Hawaii, they made up and planned the prison ministry. While we were in Hawaii, he had been calling her every afternoon and he was so sorry that he had married me. He felt trapped in our marriage. Lorna had said that she hated me because I was the one, he took out in public while she was just his sex object (lady of the night) that he snuck around with. I was devastated to hear all this and to realize that I had been so betrayed all of these years.

I went to my senior pastor who, by this time, had come onside with Paul and thought that he was doing a great job in ministry. I explained what had happened and told him that I had a tape as proof. He was mad to think that he had been duped too. We both had stuck up for Paul. I told my pastor that Paul had just left for Denver, Colorado to see his son and would be gone for about three days. My pastor said, "leave it with me, I will take care of it."

In the mean time Lorna had moved to Calgary once the news was out, she couldn't stand to face everyone. When Paul returned, the senior pastor as well as the singles pastor who had taken over from Paul were there to confront him. At first, he lied about it and then when they said there was a tape, he came clean. They told him that because of his betrayal and infidelity he had to set me free by divorcing me.

CHAPTER 24

Picking up the pieces

When I moved out Paul told them that he didn't want to be there and said that I could take what ever I wanted. One of the pastors from the church and some friends helped me move out. I moved to a little bachelor suite on 5th Ave near the City Hospital. All I took was two end tables and a wing back chair. I bought a small couch that pulled out into a bed and a table with a couple of chairs. My suite was one room and a bathroom. Here I would lick my wounds and try to come to terms with all that had happened. I prayed to God to show me what was next. The economy had taken a downturn while I was gone on the ship so getting a full-time job at the hospital was out of the question. I did however land a casual job at City Hospital but I knew that wouldn't cut it so I fell back on my barbering abilities and opened a barbershop just down the street. I had to start with a zero clientele but before long I was doing a great business. I had several people from my church become customers and my shop was in a great location.

One day, I got a call from my youngest daughter saying that she wanted to come back to Saskatoon and could she stay with me until she found work and a place to live. I said certainly. She was only with me for about two weeks and then she had landed a job as an Xray Tech at the university hospital and she had found an apartment that she liked.

Soon after I found a bigger suite for myself. I was getting pretty lonely so I decided to get a bird for a pet. I was never ever going to get involved with another man so my pet bird Joey would be my companion. I got him as a chick and, as far as he was concerned, I was his mother and we were a flock of two. He was very possessive and wanted to be everywhere that I was. I didn't want to leave him at home all by himself all day so I got another cage and kept it at the shop. He would be my mascot at the shop. My routine was that I always stopped at A&W in the morning on the way to the shop for coffee and toast. I got a small carrier for Joey, it was about the size of a lunchbox, and I made a cover for it. In the morning I would put him on the rim of the box, tap the box and say, "get in the box." He would tap the box with his beak and say, "get in the box." When we got to the A&W I would take him in and set him on the chair next to me. Because he was covered and in the dark, he never made a sound. I'm sure everyone just thought that was my lunch for work. When I got to work, I would put him in his cage which was hanging from the ceiling, that was so little kids couldn't be rough with him. He was quite the novelty for both young and old. He could whistle *Oh Canada, Heigh Ho! Heigh Ho! It's off to work I go*, and he would play peek-a-boo with the kids. He also had quite the vocabulary and would love to interact with me. I'm sure he thought that he was a human.

One day I decided to have a soaking bubble bath to soothe my aching muscles for it had been a very busy day at work. I brought Joey into the bathroom with me and set him on the vanity so he could watch himself in the mirror and be entertained. You see, if he wasn't in the same room with me, he would freak out and start screeching his head off. I settled into the tub full of bubbles and it felt oh so good. When Joey got tired of the mirror, he jumped down onto the foot edge of the tub and was fascinated with the shiny popping bubbles. I no sooner thought to myself "you wouldn't dare," he jumped into the tub thinking that he could land on the bubbles, not realizing that he would go right through them. I sat up quickly and started scooping up water in my hands frantically before he would drown. All of a sudden, I had him in my hands, a mass of bubbles surrounded him, two eyes showing through and he was sputtering and coughing with bubbles coming from his mouth. As you can imagine, he never tried that again.

CHAPTER 25

The sun shines again

Out of all my clientele, there was one man named Bob who piqued my interest. He showed up in about my second or third day in business. Not that that was odd but the fact that he was living in his mother-in-law's basement suite when his wife of thirty-two years had kicked him out, that I found odd. In most cases a mother would side with her daughter and for that reason only, would not carry on a relationship with her daughter's ex-husband. This was a sign to me that this guy must be a very special guy. I felt very sorry for this man as he poured out his life story to me. I even gave him books to help him get back to his wife, but that never happened and eventually she wrote him a letter saying that they were done and for him to get on with his life.

Things were going well for me; the shop was booming and I had a wonderful clientele. My daughters (Kathy and Tracey) were both in Saskatoon and they were such a support for me. They would drop in and visit with me at the shop whenever they could. I always had the coffee on for them and my customers. Joey was a drawing card too, especially with the kids and seniors.

I started looking forward to when Bob would show up for a haircut. He worked up north for two weeks at a time but on his two weeks off he would come in again for a haircut. We became really good friends through all the conversations we had while I cut his hair over the years and one day, he asked me to go for coffee. I turned him down then and several more times stating that I was not interested in going out or getting into another relationship, especially since he had told me that he was a recovered alcoholic and that he worked in road construction. I wasn't going down that road since my Dad was an alcoholic and he was in road construction. You see, I was trying to put him into the same box when in fact he was a totally different man. I know that I hurt Bob terribly when I said these things and it surprised me that he kept coming back.

One day when I looked into his eyes, he looked especially lonely and forlorn. I had such compassion and love for him that when he got out of the chair to go and had his hand on the door ready to open it, I said, "would you like to go for coffee?" He hesitated, and I thought to myself, MaryAnn, what have you done?

Then he turned around and with a big smile said, "yes." After cutting his hair for three and a half years, we finally went out for coffee. I realized then that he was my best friend. We had talked about everything to each other, the good, the bad and the ugly. He knew me and I knew him. There would be no surprises. He was a man of integrity.

Things progressed quite quickly and in November we got engaged and then married in the following March of 1995. He had restored my faith in humanity and I knew that we would have a great life together.

A funny thing happened while we were planning our wedding. We decided to get married quietly outside at English

Bay in Vancouver. My sister and her guy were going to stand up for us. We wanted to do it this way so that the kids from both sides wouldn't be put in an uncomfortable situation as they hadn't met yet. There had been a contest on the radio for small businesses to nominate one of their best employees, by doing a write up on them and the best one would win a trip for two by train for anywhere in Canada. I wrote up an article on my employee, Joey the bird, and how he was such an asset to my business. You guessed it! I won!!! So, Bob and I went out to Vancouver by train to get married. It was a lovely scenic trip and our marriage was wonderful.

We had rented a condo in a high rise not far from my shop and settled into our married life together when we got back. It was a beautiful place, even had a hot tub and a swimming pool. We spent a lot of time in the pool when Bob was home.

Bob tried so hard to befriend Joey, he even built him a beautiful house and yard set up but Joey just never accepted him. As far as Joey was concerned, we were a flock of two not three.

After a few months of Bob going up north for two weeks at a time every month, I thought, this is the pits, we should be together. At our age life is too short to spend so much time apart, so the next time he came home, I said, "you know if there was a job for me up north, I would put my shop up for sale and move up there with you."

Funny thing, the next time he came home he said there was a job for me up north. Not surprising because he was one of the owners of the business, Points North Landing. He was in a partnership with three brothers and once more that told me something about him as a person of integrity. How many people could handle a partnership with three brothers, you know the saying "blood is thicker than water." I told Bob that I would put my shop up for sale and if it sold within two weeks, I would be free to move up there. Funny thing is that I always told my kids that if I ever moved anywhere it would be south where it was warm, you see, I was always cold and never seemed to be able to warm up. Love makes you do very funny things.

I put an ad in the Saskatoon Star Phoenix and then continued on as usual. It was the second last day before my two weeks were up and I was thinking that the move perhaps wasn't in God's plan for my life and maybe that meant that I should scrap the idea. My next customer of that day would change everything. As he sat down in my chair he asked if I was MaryAnn McLean and I said yes that was my maiden name, but it was Westgard now. He said, "I took my barbering course with you, eons ago." When he told me his name, I realized that yes, he was in my class, but he had changed so much that I would never have known him. As we chatted while I was cutting his hair, he told me that he had moved to Calgary after school and set up a ten-chair shop. He had just retired and moved back to Saskatoon a few months ago. He said retirement wasn't what he thought it would be and he wished that he had a smaller two-chair shop where he could hire someone full time and he could come in and out whenever he wanted just to keep involved a little. I said, "Well, this is your lucky day because I have my shop up for sale. It would be perfect for you; did you see it listed in the paper?" He said that he hadn't. To make a long story short, he came back the next day, which was exactly two weeks from when I listed my shop, and we signed the papers and the deal was made. Doesn't God work in amazing ways?

CHAPTER 26

Points North

Three brand new mobile homes were purchased, Norm and Merle's, ours, and another one that I believe was to be resold when it got up north. Norman (one of Bob's partners) and his wife Merle had been living up there already and were replacing the trailer they had been living in. The insurance company had said that we could only load the mobile homes very sparingly, and only over the wheels where there was more stability since the roads up north were very bad. We had a whole home to move so we loaded our mobile home to the hilt and had to forego insuring it. To move everything by truck would have been very expensive along with the delivery of the mobile home too. Why send the mobile home up empty? When the mobile homes left Saskatoon, we prayed and prayed that everything would be okay. Points North is just west of Wollaston Lake in northern Saskatchewan so that gives you an idea of how far it was from Saskatoon. It was raining most of the way which didn't help any.

It was interesting because when the mobile homes arrived up north, they were covered in mud but of the three mobile homes, ours was in the best condition, as good as new. Our prayers answered. The other two had some cracks in the walls and the toilets had come off. The bolts had twisted right off in one case. The trucker that pulled ours up just happened to be a Christian and he said he prayed all the way up because he had never hauled a mobile home loaded like that. After the fact, he said it must have been because it was loaded that it didn't bounce around as much and there was more stability.

Once we got the outside of our home steam cleaned it was good as new. Later Bob built on a porch and a sun room. We had a beautiful home inside and out. It didn't take long to settle in and start this new life up north. Even Joey was happy.

We worked twelve-hour shifts, Bob sometimes more. We ate all our meals in the dining room in the camp setting, which was quite nice since there were excellent cooks working up there. Bob was in charge of all the construction part of things, building roads and runways and keeping all the equipment running. At one point he had over two hundred men he was responsible for and had crews working all over the place even at MacLean Lake Uranium Mine. I worked in the air terminal building, checking passengers and freight coming in and going out and also ran a souvenir gift shop in the same building. Everyone worked two weeks in and two weeks out, we did the same. On our weeks off we would usually fly down to Saskatoon to do our business, see the kids and sometimes go to Watrous or Moose Jaw Spas.

After one of our trips to Saskatoon, I bought Bob a husky malemute dog for Father's Day, his name was Kody and he was huge. If he stood up and put his paws on Bob's shoulders, his head towered over Bob's. They would become very close friends and Kody would turn out to be the best bear chaser ever which made him very popular in camp. Any bear that entered camp would soon be shown the way out. Kody was in his element and everyone loved him. When we got him, he came with a big dog house and a nice big pen which went around the dog house. This was perfect for up north. We let him run loose all day and then at night we would say good night and he would go into his pen, wait for the gate to be closed and then he'd go into the dog house for the night. This had been the ritual he followed with his previous owner and it was perfect for the north because we worried that perhaps the wolves would entice him out and kill him. At night when I finished my shift and it was dark and cold, I would call Kody and say, "Come on boy, let's go home." All of a sudden, he would come up out of the snow, shake the snow off and start running for home. He always had to beat me home. When I got there, he would be standing in his enclosure waiting for me to lock him in.

The owners would take turns staying up at Points North over Christmas with a skeleton crew. I think it was 1997 when it was our turn, and Bob being the nice guy that he was, invited all my kids and their families up to spend Christmas with us. That was the best Christmas that I had ever had to that point. Everyone loved it and the weather that year was phenomenal. We took snowmobiles and went out to a little lake where we had a wiener roast on Christmas Eve with sunshine and temperature of -4 degrees. It was the most beautiful winter wonderland and we were sharing it together. It was such a happy time and I have many other fond memories of our time at Points North Landing.

We got to be really good friends with Norm and Merle because we were the only people living up north on a permanent basis. They both worked in finance and had offices built upstairs in the hangar building. Sometimes we went out to the fishing lodge that Bob and the brothers had shares in at Pasfield Lake. We would go by float plane, do a little fishing and visiting and then come home. It was on one such trip with them that we ran into something we sure didn't want to see. Upon arrival at the lodge, we found that a bear had been inside and he had trashed everything. I never saw such a mess in my life. He had gotten into the cupboards and there was flour mixed with pancake syrup and you name it on the floor. He had bitten into canned goods and pop cans spilling contents all over. He had eaten bags of chocolate bars and even a large bottle of Tums. He had tracked everything all over the place, there were paw prints everywhere. He must have been one sick bear with all that he consumed. The lodge was generally boarded up between guests but apparently one window hadn't been boarded up and that was how he got in. It took us the whole day to clean up the mess and get things presentable again. We had to leave the next day so we didn't get much fishing in but we had quite the memory.

Another trip out to Pasfield Lake with Norm and Merle and another couple of friends, Bob and Fran from Camrose, Alberta is permanently etched in my mind. It was spring and we were going out to open the lodge to get things ready for the onslaught of guests. When we got there, the men were busy getting the boats ready, putting the motors on, etc. We girls decided to go do a little fishing and we went down to the old dock so we wouldn't be in their way. Fran got chilly and decided to go back up to the cabin while Merle and I thought we would make a few more casts from the dock. We made one more cast and the dock broke and we both went flying into the water. Surprisingly the water wasn't that cold and it was fairly shallow so we stood up and laughed like crazy, while looking like a couple of drowned rats. I said, "Well we might just as well fish from here." Just as Merle was getting out of the water, I made one more cast and had a big fish on my line, as I was reeling it in, I noticed a whole bunch of fish on the bottom just laying sunning themselves on the sand by my feet. I had the fish that I reeled in still hanging from my rod and I reached down with my bare hands and grabbed one of those big fish behind the gills and pulled it out of the water. I couldn't believe it, but I had caught a fish with my bare hands and that is no lie. We teased the guys later, saying that we didn't need a boat we could catch them by hand. We all had a good laugh about it and that story has been told over and over through the years. We had my two fish for supper that night but everyone had caught their limit and Fran ended up catching her first fish ever and it was the biggest of the day.

Points North Landing was at the end of the road, from here freight and people were flown the rest of the way into their communities. Bob looked after the ice roads in winter and one time he took me with him when he was checking the roads. He took me across Lake Athabasca in the winter time on the ice road and I remember the weird feeling that I had when we were halfway across and I couldn't see land anywhere and wondering how deep the water was under the ice. It was very scary but I was in good hands, Bob was very experienced and I knew that he knew what he was doing and how to do it.

One day, on one of my days off, Bob asked if I wanted to see what Cigar Lake Mine was like. He had arranged a tour for us. We even got to go underground and, let me tell you, that was quite the experience. On the way down in the cage I experienced the blackest black that I have ever seen, there wasn't a glimmer of light anywhere. However, when we got to the bottom and the door opened there were fluorescent lights everywhere making it so bright and cheery. It didn't feel like you were underground at all. It was a very educational tour and I certainly learned a lot.

Through my job up north I met lots of very interesting people from all over the world. There would be people coming from France, Germany and other European countries checking out the nearby uranium mines, people from the States coming up to go fishing in the pristine lakes of northern Saskatchewan plus the indigenous locals coming and going. In winter we would sometimes see dog sleds come and go through camp. Sometimes dog sled teams would be shipped on one of the DC3's to go to races. They didn't want the dogs to be tired when they started the race.

CHAPTER 27

Our acreage

After five years up north, I was beginning to see that my mom and stepfather were getting up in years and I was worried about them. I knew that they could really use some help. I expressed my concerns to Bob and he said that we should move to Camrose to look after them and he could commute from there up to Points North until his retirement. The next time that we went out for our two weeks off, we drove from Saskatoon to Camrose and started looking for a place to live. After having all the space and freedom that we had while living up north, we decided that we should look for an acreage within about ten or fifteen minutes outside of Camrose. That would be better for our dog Kody too. We looked at three acreages and settled on one that we thought would be perfect. It was just listed that day. We gave a deposit with intention to buy but we needed a couple of weeks to sell our mobile home up north.

Now this is where we had to trust God to work things out. Two weeks wasn't very long to pull it all together especially since Bob had to be in Regina for part of that time in some important meetings. Rosalie, the head of the Education department in Wollaston had expressed that she wanted to get a mobile home like ours, so Bob immediately got on the phone and told her that ours was for sale. She came and saw it and wanted it on condition that Bob could deliver it from Points North to Wollaston over the ice road before the ice went out. He agreed and left for his meetings in Regina. In the meantime, I packed everything and he had told his workers from the shop to move all our possessions into the wood shop till it could be freighted south. Then I moved into the employee housing in the camp.

When Bob got back, he took off the porch and sunroom and got a flatbed trailer which he had to weld extra wings onto, to add length and width. Then he and a couple of his men loaded the trailer that night and planned to leave first thing in the morning. Meanwhile he got a call from the insurance company saying that they wouldn't insure the mobile home because of the time of year and the fact that the trip was too risky.

The next day was Easter Sunday. It was +9 degrees and the ice was rubbery with several inches of water on top. Bob asked if I wanted to go along. I said, "I think you need someone to stay home and pray." It was quite the convoy when they left. The truck with the mobile home, another with the porch and sunroom, two loaders to unload at the other end and Bob in his half-ton. He gave his guys very strict orders on how to drive, how fast to go, and where to go. About halfway there they found that a truck loaded with lumber had gone through the ice with just the top sticking out. There was a man standing on top waving his hands and a woman was walking on the ice. Bob radioed his men not to stop because that may put them in the same position, but rather continue on at four miles per hour. Meanwhile Bob picked up the woman in his half-ton and radioed for help from Wollaston to get the man. They had been drinking and were definitely going too fast. Bob's crew made it safely unloaded and headed for home, arriving late that night. The next day, Department of Highways closed the road. Once again, we had witnessed God's work in our lives.

We moved to the acreage in the early spring of 2000. It was a beautiful acreage, just right in that it was only ten minutes from town and yet we had space and privacy. The previous owner had been boarding two horses for a man from town named Grant. He was a roper and would win occasionally in rodeo events. We told him that whatever agreement he had had with the previous owner, we would continue to honour that, besides it was kind of nice to have the horses on the property. We loved our time on the acreage and we made some very nice friendships with our neighbours.

Mom and Ed were very happy to have us there. I think it took some of the worry out of their lives. Bob and Ed really hit it off and became real good friends which really pleased Mom and I. We did a lot of things together when Bob was home from Points North. Mom had formed a band called "Ilyne's Band" which played at the Senior Homes in Camrose. Almost immediately she recruited Bob to come play with them. She played piano, Bob played banjo and there were several other instruments besides. Mom always said that she had to go play for the old folks and in most cases, she was older than them.

We got to see more of Bob's kids while living at the acreage because it was more of a central location. We had a lot of fun when any of the kids would come. We had a pool table and shuffleboard in the family room so that was a hit. One Christmas we took everyone skating on the little lake in the middle of Camrose. In the summer we had two great big gardens and the kids liked getting raw veggies. We also had raspberries, saskatoon berries and strawberries.

When we moved to the acreage it was early spring. Bob happened to be up north when it was time to rototill the gardens and he told me to hire someone from town to do it. The guy came out but couldn't get his blades to go through the hard dirt, it was like concrete. When Bob got home, he got a load of sand and then used the abundance of horse manure we had around, put it on and then rototilled with the new rototiller that he bought from town. When he got through, the soil was just perfect for planting and we had one of the best veggie crops ever.

Looking back, I am so amazed at what we were able to accomplish on that acreage. When Bob was home, he built me a green house to start plants in, he built a sun room onto the house, he got two of his brothers to come and put a new steel roof on the barn, and he revamped his shop by putting in a large automatic door so he could get larger pieces of equipment inside. He finished off the basement of our house and put a hot tub in. He was amazing! And he did all that while still fixing peoples' tractors, farm equipment, etc., building a ramp for the neighbours so that their paraplegic son could come home to visit them and doing anything else for whomever. Most of this he did without pay, he just liked helping people.

While he was doing all of this, I got a job at Battle River school division driving a school bus as a spare driver and later moved on to Transportation Supervisor, a job that I really liked. I put in one hour in the morning when the school buses would arrive to the high school and then one hour later in the afternoon when the school buses would leave again and I would get paid for six hours because they had to call me in twice. This worked out really well with my being caregiver to Mom and Ed. When Ed gave up his driver's licence, I would drive them to appointments, etc., I also took out a licence to cut hair for seniors in their homes. All of this was done while still managing the acreage since Bob was away a lot. I had two huge gardens, nine flower beds, grass to cut and hedges to trim. I planted fruit trees and put in many rose bushes and perennials. For a while I took in animals from the humane society that needed homes until they got their forever home. We ended up keeping three dogs and three cats. The grandkids sure loved playing with them when they came to visit.

We never really put down roots in Camrose because we didn't plan on staying there. We figured that by Mom and Ed's ages, we would be there maybe at best ten years. It turned out to be nine years. In the meantime, we were really good friends with Bob and Fran who had been childhood friends with Bob and had moved to Alberta from the Kyle area in Saskatchewan. They had so much in common with each other and would spend a lot of time reminiscing about old times. We also had a good relationship with our neighbours just north of us, the ones that Bob built the ramp for.

One summer we accepted a chance to go with LAMP (Lutheran Association of Missionaries and Pilots). We spent two weeks up in northern Manitoba with Al and Darlene Anderson teaching Vacation Bible School to the native kids up there. Because of our previous experience with the north, we felt quite at home in northern Manitoba. We left there more blessed than we had blessed them.

CHAPTER 28 - RETIREMENT

After Mom and Ed had passed on, we were trying to figure where to retire and we were throwing out all kinds of ideas. Soon after we took a trip down to Medicine Hat and Colleen my daughter-in-law said, "Do you want to see where I work? I'll take you on a tour." We went and Bob was so impressed with the retirement home, but I not so much because I didn't think I was ready for that kind of living yet. However, on a later trip down to Medicine Hat he booked an appointment for a full-blown tour with one of the salesmen. After that tour, especially after seeing the courtyard, I said, "Where do I sign?" We went into the office and put our names on a waiting list. Alvin Kurpjuweit explained to us that if we took a one-bedroom suite first the waiting wouldn't be so long and then we could try for a two-bedroom suite once we were in and have first preference over someone from the outside. That sounded okay to us.

Once back home we started fixing things up to sell our acreage, not that it was in bad shape, because it wasn't. We stained the deck, and painted the barn, corrals and all of the out buildings just to freshen things up. Things were looking so nice, so we called a realtor and put the place up for sale. No sooner had we done that then we had a terrible wind and hail storm go through which wrecked many roofs and took out all the windows in the greenhouse. The fences and deck were pitted from the hail, it was a real mess. At least we knew that our insurance would cover everything. The for sale sign was removed and we started all over again. I think God was slowing us down because we were moving too fast and not waiting for His timing. We had thought that if the acreage sold and we still didn't have a place in Chinook Village we would rent somewhere until we could get in and that would have meant two moves instead of one which was not the best. Once everything was fixed up, the for sale sign went back up, but now it was fall and not a good time to be trying to sell. Finally, in late November Bob found someone who wanted to buy, it wasn't even the realtor but Bob on his own who found a buyer.

The day we came home from signing the papers, we were in the house less than ten minutes when the phone rang and it was Chinook Village saying that they had a one-bedroom suite in the Lane Building if we wanted it. We said yes, sight unseen, and drove down to give a deposit and see what we had gotten. It was very nice but small. We chose what colour we wanted it painted and what colour carpets, etc., and then we left. We were glad when we found out later, that the value of our acreage had gone up during the time when we were fixing everything up the second time. The storm had made us money in the long run. God knew what was best for us and allowed those things to happen to slow us down and wait for His timing.

Back home we had so much to do. We had to clean out all the out buildings and downsize big time. It was winter so a garage sale was not in the picture. We took things to Emergency Housing and the Salvation Army and Bob took many, many, loads to the dump. We found great homes for our animals. We packed and then we went up to Edmonton to look after Bob's daughter's cats while they went on a vacation.

As soon as they got back, we went out to Kelowna to look after another of Bob's daughter and her husband's alpacas, dogs, and cat while they went away on holidays. When they got home, we left for home to meet the movers and have them load up our stuff to take to Medicine Hat. When we got to the Hat, we stayed at my daughter's place while she was away and babysat her two kids. Once she got home, we went to our suite in Chinook Village. Our stuff was piled sky high with only a small walk way around the boxes. We looked at each other and agreed that we had to downsize some more. No problem, it's just stuff. We were so happy that we were finally here. What a whirlwind way to get here. By the way, we moved in on the coldest day of the year, the temperature was -31.

CHAPTER 28

Chinook Village

It didn't take long to realize that we had made the right move. The neighbours that we had on our floor were so friendly and accepted us immediately. Jeanette Wolfer invited us over to her place to get to know the others from our floor. This immediately felt like home.

Before long Bob was asked if he would let his name stand for the upcoming elections as a Board Member at the next AGM. He agreed and was voted in. He would spend the next ten years as a Board Member.

I was so happy to have two of my kids and their families here in Medicine Hat, but I was in for a very big shock when in two years later, my son Bill would die without warning, of a heart attack. I would have never seen that coming, he had just been to the doctor for his annual check up and all was okay. You never expect your child to die before you. I was heart broken when I got the news. We had just stopped in at his place on our way to the Senior Games in Calgary and we were sitting on the deck with him and his wife Colleen enjoying a cup of tea when he asked if Bob would help him build a fence because their fence was rotting. Bob said sure, next time you're off we can get started. We went on our way and Monday morning Bill left for work in Weyburn. He took his trailer so he could stay in the campground there. The night before he died, he called me and was very up beat. We talked for a long time, having one of the best conversations we had ever had and at the end of our conversation he said, "Mom, I sure love you," and I said, "I love you too and I'm so proud of you." He was a real hard-working family man, with wife and kids that loved him. The next day he would be found dead in his trailer with the T.V. going, lying on his bed, with a bowl of cereal on his chest. He never showed up for work. Initially I was mad then angry. Before long, I gave myself a reality check and decided to look at the pluses. I had seen him grow up, get married, have children, I saw the man that he had become and I thought of all those people that don't get that opportunity. Some lose their children as babies. God gave him to me for forty-eight wonderful years, what a blessing, and his last words to me were of him expressing his love for me. What more could a mother want?

Now to tell you once again of Bob's character, he went to Weyburn to bring back Bill's trailer and he was adamant that he was going to build that fence, which he did with the help of Bill's friend Rob. This once again shows Bob's integrity. When he says he'll do something, he does it.

When we first arrived in Medicine Hat, we went church shopping, tried about three churches but didn't have a good feel about any of them. They seemed cliquey and not friendly at all. One day we were at A&W having breakfast and there were about six guys at a table near us. They were laughing and joking around when one of the guys came over and asked if we were new to Medicine Hat and we said, "yes." Then he asked if we were Christians and I thought, how do you know, do we have it written on our foreheads or something. We said, "yes." Then he invited us to come to his church, Hillcrest Evangelical Church. The next Sunday we went to try it out and were accepted at once. We even got invited out for lunch with a group of people. It wasn't long after that we became members of Hillcrest.

We were so happy to have decided to make Medicine Hat our place of retirement. We loved the milder climate and the fact that we had more time to do some of the things that we could never do before because we were too busy. Bob played senior slow pitch ball and just loved it. He also loved to curl and joined the Senior Curling League. I played Pickleball and just loved it. We both got involved in senior athletics with the Alberta Senior Games and the 55+ Senior Games where we had a lot of fun and met a lot of people. I also entered my photography in some of these events. We enjoyed every moment of our lives together and had so much fun.

Bob was asked to come out to sing barbershop and he so enjoyed that. It is through Bob's barbershop singing that we met and made lasting friends with Gord and Sherry Nott. I sang with the Harmonettes for a while and Bob sang in the Chinook Village Choir.

One day I was asked if I would help one of the ladies here at Chinook create a newsletter for Chinook Village residents. It wasn't long before she turned the paper over to me. She was in her eighties, had just recently lost two of her brothers and was having some health problems. I have been doing the paper for almost ten years now and I believe that it is well appreciated. I have fun doing it too. Not sure how much longer I can do it. I guess that's up to God.

We have enjoyed living here at Chinook Village and enjoyed getting involved with all the goings on. Bob and I have been a great team together. We have loved dressing up and acting goofy at the various functions. Perhaps living our childhood now.

After five years of battling cancer, I lost my best friend on October 15, 2019. We knew what was coming and we talked about it at length. The reality is, when you grow old it isn't likely that you and your spouse will go together unless you are in a car crash or something like that. One of you will be left alone. I know that I will survive, I have lived alone before and with God I can do it again. I am so thankful that Bob suggested that we move into Chinook Village because this is the best place that I could ever be as a widow. I have family and friends close by.

I don't want people to feel sorry for me when they read this story, I want them to see the power of God and how He worked in my life even when I rejected Him.

Before I leave you, I would like to tell you about some things that have helped me through my life.

1. **Attitude** – Our attitude is more important than the circumstance. Phil 2:5. With the right attitude we can endure anything.

2. **The Vertical** – (our relationship with God) is more important than the horizontal (our relationship with man).

3. **The Long Term** – is more important than the short term. Short term is like a snowflake in the hot sun. Long term is eternal life with God.

4. **What We Have** – is more important than what we don't have. The very poorest in Canada are considered rich in the eyes of the people in a third world country.

Isaiah 43:18-20

One of my favourite passages tells of God making an oasis out of a desert. Just as He made an oasis out of a desert, He wants to bring life and beauty into our lives, if only we will let him.

Here are some poems that I wrote shortly after my conversion experience in 1979. I was so full of gratitude that He would accept me after the twenty-five years that I had rejected Him.

My Blessings

The Lord has blessed me richly
It's amazing just how much
He loved and forgave me
My soul He then did touch

He opened my eyes to see myself
My self pity it was gone
He gave me strength and power
And the will to carry on

The sun is brighter in the sky
The earth, a soft warm brown
The trees took on new beauty
And love sprang up all around

People all look different now
Their faces seem to shine
When I can see the good in them
It makes me feel just fine

Praise to you, dear Lord
You're all I knew you would be
A beam of love and kindness
Directed at the likes of me

You've done so much to help
me grow
You've watered me with care
You've trimmed away the worst
in me
Replacing your love there

I thank you Lord and praise
your name
I know not how or why
You'd pick a sinner such as me
To bless up to the sky

More Poems

My Meditations

While sitting on the riverbank
One afternoon in prayer
The whole world seemed
so awesome
My life so small a share

The vastness of the universe
The sweetness of the air
I know that God is close to me
I can see Him everywhere

He is in the song of all the birds
He is in the rustling trees
He is in the creepy crawly things
And He is in the likes of me

I know where I am going
Because I do believe
With faith and trust in God alone
I'll never need to grieve

I'll try my very hardest
To do my very best
For it's only in the doing
That each soul can be blest

Love for God

No matter what some people say
I'll love my God all the way
He gives me strength when I
am weak
To, help me turn the other cheek

No matter if the sun should lose
its ray
I'll love my God all the way
I'll trust in Him for He is light
With Him I can know that all
is right

No matter if the worst was done
I would love my God till
Kingdom come
For He saved me when I was lost
His only son the price it cost

NO matter if I face torture
and death
I'll love my God with my
last breath
For He loved me, a wretched soul
Lost and descending out
of control

God Bless